Saints, Our Friends and Teachers

Fun and Easy Activities

SAINTS
Our Friends & Teachers
Fun & Easy Activities

LEE PALENCAR

TWENTY
THIRD 23rd
PUBLICATIONS

Dedication

For my parents, Leonard and Sara Mattano

Twenty-Third Publications
A Division of Bayard
185 Willow Street
P.O. Box 180
Mystic, CT 06355
(860) 536-2611 or (800) 321-0411
www.twentythirdpublications.com

ISBN:1-58595-511-6
Library of Congress Catalog Card Number: 2005923884
Printed in the U.S.A.

Contents

Introduction

Welcome!

If friends are people who care about us, can offer advice to help us better ourselves, are good listeners, and are able to speak for us, then saints are our friends!

When children are very young, the stories of the saints' lives can become real for them. The events in the lives of these extraordinarily ordinary people can have a lifetime impact on children. If children are introduced to the saints as an integral part of their lives, they tend to carry this into adulthood—in fact, throughout their lives.

This book offers information and ideas for celebrating the lives of saints, especially those relevant in some way to children. Many include the saints as children themselves—those kidnapped and enslaved, those asked to perform extraordinary acts, and those who led quiet outward lives but wonderfully full and secret interior lives.

You can use the suggestions to introduce a lesson, reinforce one, or incorporate the saint into your lesson plan. In each case they enhance but do not replace the lesson. The material on the saints should help you meet your objectives, not distract from them.

The abundant material for each saint includes the following:

- reasons why the particular choices, actions, or events in a saint's life could positively influence young children;

- a variety of objectives;

- an explanation of various symbols for each saint;

- suggestions for presenting the saint and adding creative touches to the characters;

- the Story or Dialogue, which may be read or acted out using the saint figures;

- a prayer to encourage children to learn about intercession and how to apply the important aspects of a particular saint to their own lives;

- vocabulary words.

Saints are God's gift to all of us. By following their example, we can become more and more like Jesus. Introducing young children to holiness is a gift that will remain with them throughout their lives.

General Teaching Instructions

Catechists can feel free to use the material in this book in the way best suited to their needs and those of their group.

Here are some suggestions:

1. Read the story and discuss it. Make the figures (or have the children make them), talk about the symbols and lessons to be learned. Have the children take the figures home.

2. Make the figures by yourself or with the children. Act the story out using the figures, following the simple directions provided within each story.

3. Make the saint figures and read some of the introductory material. Do further research on the saint and share that with the children. Older children can do the research themselves.

4. Invite the children to make or draw the figures. They can punch holes at the top and tie a ribbon to hang the figures. Or they can glue small magnets to the back. The children can then offer the figures as gifts to seniors, the sick or shut-ins, other children, their own families.

5. Read the story. Make the saint and other figures, and invite the children to tell their own versions of the story.

6. If you are really ambitious, think about making your own foam book of saints. Use the larger format and thicker foam (or construction paper) for the "sheets." Large rings, purchased at office supply stores, can hold all the pages together once you've punched holes in them. Create backgrounds (like the grotto in Bernadette), and glue the saints and other characters within scenes. Or, using hook and loop tape, have the children put saints and other characters in the right place as you tell the stories of the saints. You can also use sheets of felt and glue felt backing onto the figures. It's all great fun!

Frequently evaluate your presentation. How did it affect the children? Were they engaged? Bored? Talkative about the subject? Or talkative about other things? Did they like the crafting but not the story? Did they prefer to be involved in acting out the story? Did they improvise along the lines of the story? When you plan, use the material in this book as a jumping-off point. Keep in mind that the more specific you are with your goals, the more efficiently you'll teach. You will be able to better evaluate the experience for future adaptations.

Of course we know that different groups of children have their own preferences and characteristics. What works with some may not work at all with others. Keep track of what works. If you have a particularly rowdy group and acting out the story stirs them up too much, keep them busy making the characters while you talk about the saint. If you have a very shy group, perhaps acting out the story with the figures would draw them out.

Often the activity does not go as planned. If the children seem to be pulling you in another direction and it does not conflict with faith formation, then try it. The Holy Spirit may be speaking through them to you!

General Craft Instructions

Have fun with these saints figures! You might think you are not a craftsperson and that creating these characters with foam is difficult, but it is truly a fun and easy project. Foam is a very forgiving medium, easy to cut, glue, and push into shape. You will find craft foam at craft stores and often in the craft sections or stationery sections of department or discount stores. Undoubtedly, the shapes will not fit perfectly, but that's okay. The figures are handmade and should not look like die cut figures.

For those who cannot or prefer not to use foamboard, heavy construction paper will do. Most of the directions given here will work for construction paper also. There is also another, very simple way to make the figures. Copy the complete outline of whichever saints and accompanying figures you will need. Let the children color them in and cut them out. They can glue popsicle sticks on the back so they can hold the figures. Or they can punch holes at the top to tie ribbons for hanging them.

Following are some guidelines that will help turn the activity of working with foam or other mediums into a wonderful, stress-free experience. Share these directions with older children who can make the figures themselves.

1. Cut out pattern pieces and place the pieces into an envelope so nothing is lost or mixed up with other characters. Label the envelopes with the characters' names.

2. Place each pattern piece face down onto the backside of the foam. I use the 2mm thickness. There are beautiful colors available in any craft store.

3. Trace around each pattern piece with a mechanical pencil for a fine line. But if you prefer a black marker, then use what works for you. Feel free to experiment.

4. Carefully cut around each foam piece. Cut directly on the pencil lines and try to keep your scissors perpendicular to the foam edge. Using sharp, large scissors to make long slicing motions leaves fewer jagged edges.

5. Be sure to mark the back of each foam piece with an "X" so you can tell it's the back when it is time to glue. This is important! You'd be surprised how difficult it is to tell the back from the front. If you forget to mark the back, compare the foam piece to the completed line drawing next to the pattern pieces to see which shape is correct.

6. Draw facial features with a mechanical pencil. You may use the pattern or the finished foam character for feature ideas. If the foam color is very light, you can hold the pattern piece underneath the foam with a strong light (or use a light box) behind to trace the features. This doesn't work with darker foam colors. Otherwise, just draw the face you'd like to see. You can also draw free hand with markers.

7. Use craft paints or fine-line permanent markers to add color and detail. Doing it at this point allows you to make another face in case the features don't turn out as you like. Let the paint dry thoroughly. Permanent markers work the best for indicating facial features. Craft paint is good, too, but markers allow more freedom. Use a color slightly darker than the facial color for the nose and eyelids. When you have the eye color in place and dry, place a tiny dot of black paint or permanent marker in the

center of the iris, then use a tiny bit of white paint either just left or just right of the pupil. This adds dimension to the eye. Putting a tiny bit of darkish pink on the cheeks, then rubbing with your finger to blend, adds a bit of blush to the cheeks. The foam absorbs metallic markers and they leave only a dull color behind. Acrylic iridescent gold paint works beautifully and can be cleansed with water.

8. Assemble pieces, as indicated on the example, on another piece of foam, which is the backing. Leave enough room for all the pieces. This backing should not be cut to fit yet. Wait until all the pieces are glued on first. Always put the pieces in place once or twice before gluing.

9. Glue with white glue or hot glue, holding each piece as necessary for them to fit well together. Be careful not to re-wet any painted areas. Remove any excess glue with a toothpick. Hot glue creates lots of strings, too, and it will scar the foam, so care is needed in this step. Small children should not use hot glue guns. However, if adults can apply it, hot glue dries very quickly and shortens the time needed to hold the pieces together. Using white glue is a slower process, and you may enjoy a more relaxing craft experience. You can glue pieces in layers, too. For example, for Our Lady of Guadalupe, glue the hair above the face, then glue the veil on top of the hair. Use a bit of hot glue under the top part of the veil to secure it to the foam backing. Fitting these together properly is why the dry fit is so important.

10. When all pattern pieces are dry, cut out the backing, carefully following the pattern piece edges. Hold the scissors at about a 45-degree angle. This allows the backing to "disappear" behind the character. Also, don't try to cut around each curl in the hair or each ear. Just cut inside the area; there's still enough backing to hold everything together. Two layers of foam strengthen the entire piece.

11. At this point, you may embellish the character using ribbon, flowers, charms, leaves, twigs, puff balls, stickers, paint, markers, hole punchers, decorative scissors, fabric scraps, lace, doilies, yarn, costume jewelry, beads, chenille sticks, sequins, religious medals, crosses, buttons, crucifixes, wire, gold craft paint, burlap, etc. The possibilities are unlimited. If you want to add halos to Mary or Jesus, cut an oval or circle from yellow or gold foam, or paint the foam with gold craft paint. Hot glue the halo to the back of the head after placing it where it looks best from the front. Gold wire would work, too, if you wanted a more three-dimensional look. For patches on clothing, use real fabric scraps. Add lines with a permanent marker to make "stitches" from the patch to the clothing.

12. You may want to add an adhesive-backed magnet to the back (perhaps several small pieces scattered across the back of the piece). The magnets allow you to place the figures on a magnetic board or cookie sheet to demonstrate or act out the lives of the saints. You can also punch a hole at the top of each figure and add ribbon or raffia to hang the figures on a "Saint Tree" in your meeting space or in front of the windows. If you don't want to put a hole in the saints' heads, glue a rectangle of foam to the back of the head, leaving half of the piece sticking above the head. Put your hole in that piece. You can also glue a craft stick to the bottom back of the figure so small hands

can use the saints as puppets. Perhaps you'll want to make a "Saint Place" on your bulletin board. If you're really ambitious, you can make a diorama for each saint.

Remember that these characters are intended to be hand-traced, cut out by hand, and glued by hand. Don't worry if the pieces don't fit perfectly. Feel free to add your own bits and pieces to the figures.

Note: Almost any character can be adapted for another saint. For example, if you want to make lots of children, then use the characters from one of the saints with children. You can duplicate figures, like the soldiers in Joan of Arc's army. There are also scene pieces (the boat for Saint Peter, the grotto for Saint Bernadette) which you can use to make a set.

One great lesson the saints teach us is that Jesus doesn't require perfection, just a willing heart that loves him, our Father in heaven, and the Holy Spirit. God is our loving creator, and made us in God's image. We were meant to be creative, too! So, give God your heart because the rest is art!

Saint Anthony of Padua

Why This Saint?

One of the teachings of Jesus that is most difficult to understand is giving up possessions (things we have) for the love of God. Anthony of Padua is an excellent example for children. He had so much material wealth and was fortunate by any standard. This saint's example invites children to consider how such a person could give up their wealthy way of life and still be happy.

Lessons to Be Learned

- To understand that material things are not evil, nor do they bring the happiness that we long for
- To realize that some people have far less than we do
- To discover the joy of giving to the needy
- To learn to value spiritual goods over material goods

Symbols Mark the Saint

Gifts: Young Anthony holds a gift in his hands symbolizing his wealth.

Bright clothing, jewelry, etc.: These signify the wealth of his family and the excitement the world can offer.

Monk's clothing: The subtle color contrasts sharply with the bright colors of his youth, symbolizing love of God over material things.

Using This Saint

See general instructions common to all the saints (pp.2-5).

As an alternative to *Acting Out the Story,* invite the children to reflect: how often do they talk to their friends and family about the things they want? You can ask them to keep track for a week. For example, the child may say, "I asked my parents for a new computer game twenty times this week, but I only said my prayers fourteen times." This comparison can be an eye-opener. Ask the children if they were satisfied when they finally did get what they wanted. How long did their happiness last? Usually once we have one thing, another desire "pops up." Discuss what the saints like Anthony show us: that our only true and lasting happiness lies in God.

Acting Out the Story

Figures: young Anthony, Father, Mother, Anthony the priest, other priest (optional: you might make more than one priest)

You can use the boat (p.119) from Saint Peter to reenact the boat trip in Saint Anthony's story.

If you choose to use the figures to tell the story, here are some suggestions. Either you or the children can make one or more of each of the figures and attach them to popsicle sticks or dowels. Have the children hold their characters up and put them down at the places indicated in the story. Older children might make the characters act out the "actions"; for example, where the characters in the story are walking, have the figures "walk" (move back and forth); when the characters are talking, have the figures face each other and move up and down slightly; and so on.

Story

Anthony was a rich little boy. *(Hold up young Anthony)* Anthony's rich mother and father wanted him to become a nobleman when he grew up. To be a nobleman could be a good thing. But Anthony did not want to be a nobleman. He wanted to become a priest.

(Hold up Father and Mother) "Mother and Father, I know you want me to become a nobleman and take care of people. But I believe God is asking me to be a priest," he told them one day.

(Father moves around as though upset) "What?!" his father yelled. "You want to become a priest? You will have nothing of your own. Who will take care of my land? Who will inherit all my things? I will never have any grandchildren!" Anthony's father left the room upset. *(Put down Father)*

Anthony's mother was crying. Quietly she said, "Anthony, why? Why do you want to throw all our gifts away? Don't you know that we have worked hard all our lives so you would never be in need of anything? The life of a priest is hard, lonely, and poor. Anthony, why would you hurt us so much? Have we not always been kind and loving to you?"

Why do you think Anthony wanted to give up all his riches to become poor? Would you ever think of doing that? Would you ever give up one toy, maybe even your favorite toy, to a child who had no toys? Well, that is something like what Anthony wanted to do. He wanted to give up everything he had. Even though his parents were sad, they knew that Anthony loved Jesus. He loved Jesus so much that he wanted to give up everything he had to live and love for Jesus.

(Anthony moves closer to Mother) Anthony hugged his mother and said, "Mother, I love Jesus. By giving me all this out of love, you taught me how to give to others. I want to give my life to Jesus. Please try to understand." Little by little his mother and father did understand, although they were still disappointed. *(Put down Mother and Anthony)*

(Hold up Anthony the priest) Anthony became a priest. He was a quiet man, who studied and prayed a lot. His desire was to be a missionary. A missionary is someone who wants to live in a far away land to teach people about Jesus.

(Hold up boat. Have boat and Anthony "sail") However, Anthony did not become a missionary. When he tried to go to the far away land of Morocco, he was shipwrecked. *(Put boat and Anthony down)* When he returned to his country, he chose to live in a cave. He prayed for other people. *(Hold up Anthony)* "O Jesus, I am so happy just spending all my hours with you. I never

want to do anything else." This was a good thing to do, but it was not what God wanted for Anthony. *(Put Anthony down)*

One day something happened that changed Anthony's life forever. A priest was supposed to come to the monastery to give a talk about God, but he never showed up. The other priests remembered Anthony in the cave.

(Hold up Priests) "I'll bet he knows a lot and can speak to the people about the love of Jesus," said one priest.

"Let's go ask him," said another priest, and they all went to the cave.

"Anthony!" all the priests called. "Come out. You have a mission from God."

(Hold up Anthony) Anthony stepped out from his cave and into the daylight.

"Yes, brothers," he answered, "what is the mission?"

"Come to the monastery," they said. "You need to come and speak about God." They were afraid Anthony might say no.

"Yes, I'll come, for this is what God wants," Anthony replied.

(Put down Anthony and Priests) Anthony must have found it difficult to leave the cave and enter the big monastery where the priests waited for him. When he stood up to speak, Anthony knew God's Spirit would give him the words to say.

Anthony's talk about Jesus impressed everyone so much that he was asked to speak to different groups of people. He spent the rest of his life travelling and speaking throughout Italy and France. Anthony was declared a saint in 1232. In 1946, he was named a Doctor of the Church. Many people pray to Saint Anthony because of his kindness and love.

Prayer

Dear Saint Anthony, I can't always do everything I want to do, just as you never got to Morocco. Sometimes I have to wait to know what God wants for me, like you did. Teach me to pray and love Jesus and wait to know what my gifts are. Then I can use them to love Jesus and work out of love, too, just as you did. Amen.

Words to Know

Nobleman: a rich man who takes care of the poorer people under his care

Priest: a man who gives his life to Jesus and takes care of poor people

Shipwrecked: when your boat sinks and you land somewhere you didn't plan to be

Monastery: a big house for priests

Impressed: to be "wowed" by something

Speaker: someone who talks about or explains certain things to a group of people

Inspire: to make people feel they can do anything for Jesus

Father

Mother

Anthony the priest

Other priest(s)

Saint Bathild

Why This Saint?

Centuries ago, the kidnapping of children for purposes of slavery was all too common. And it still takes place today. Introducing children to this idea might be a little scary, but the cruelty and hardships of slavery influenced the lives of many saints. Children can't help recognizing that their own lives are safer and happier. Bathild can encourage them to feel gratitude and a sense of purpose in life. She is an excellent example for making the best of a hard situation. Bathild chose to do wonderful things with her life, spending it for other people.

Symbols Mark the Saint

Scepter: This decorated stick signifies that the person holding it is the ruler.

Crown: The golden ring that fits around the top of the head, usually decorated with jewels, shows that the person wearing it is a ruler.

Lessons to Be Learned

- To better understand how some other people live
- To practice gratitude
- To instill a sense of purpose, to make something good of their lives
- To discover that God is present in all things, even hard things
- To introduce the concept of God's will as a mystery
- To accept the truth that giving is always better than keeping everything for oneself

Using This Saint

See general instructions common to all the saints (pp.2-5).

After the story, you might guide the conversation to asking the children how they think Bathild felt. Discuss Bathild's decision to do her duties well.

Acting Out the Story

Figures: young Bathild (make chains separate so you can add or take away, or make two separate figures), Mary, King Clovis, Queen Bathild, poor boy, Prince Clotaire (same as Clovis).

If you choose to use the figures to tell the story, here are some suggestions. Either you or the children can make one or more of each of the figures and attach them to popsicle sticks or dowels. Have the children hold their characters up and put them down at the places indicated in the story. Older children might make the characters act out the "actions"; for example, where the characters in the story are walking, have the figures "walk" (move back and forth); when the characters are talking, have the figures face each other and move up and down slightly; and so on.

Story

Bathild—isn't that a beautiful name? Bathild was a little girl *(Hold up Bathild without chains)* born a long, long time ago in England. But a terrible thing happened! When Bathild was still young girl, she was kidnapped. Do you know what the word "kidnap" means? It means that someone takes you away from your home and your family.

(Hold up Bathild with chains) Poor Bathild! She was very scared. She cried and cried and begged the men to take her home. "I want my mother!" Bathild cried. "Tell her to come and get me. I want to go home." But the mean men did not take her home, or let her mother or father come to get her.

(Put down Bathild) We can only imagine how frightened Bathild was. She was all alone in another country. She was sold as a slave to a man named Erkenwald. He was the mayor for the palace of King Clovis II in France. Her mother and father had no idea where she was. They would never have been able to find her.

(Hold up Bathild without chains) Bathild probably had a lot of cleaning to do in a huge castle. She washed the pots and pans until they sparkled. She scrubbed the floors until they shined. Her beds always smelled so fresh, just like her mother's.

One day the mayor Erkenwald said to her, "Bathild, you do such a good job and work hard. I am putting you in charge of the whole house." Now Bathild managed all the important affairs in the house. We can imagine that she treated others with a lot of kindness.

(Hold up Mary) "Mary, you scrubbed that floor very well," Bathild told one of the new slaves. Mary was still crying because she missed her mother. "It will be all right, Mary."

(Put down Mary and Bathild) Bathild's kindness and goodness were noticed by someone very important—King Clovis himself! Do you know what happened next?

(Hold up King Clovis and Bathild) "Bathild," said King Clovis one day. Bathild was walking in the gardens picking flowers for the dinner table. "I have fallen in love with you. I want to marry you."

Bathild was surprised and so happy! She had seen King Clovis at the castle for years and had fallen in love with him, too. They were married and were very happy. King Clovis and Queen Bathild had three sons. They were named Clotaire III, Childeric II, and Thierry I. Bathild loved them very much.

(Put down King Clovis and Queen Bathild) Now that Queen Bathild was rich, she had all the food she could eat and the most beautiful dresses to wear. Do you think she forgot about Mary or all the other poor people and slaves? No, she did not.

(Hold up King Clovis and Queen Bathild) "I remember what it was like to be kidnapped and a slave, Clovis," she told her husband. "Please do not allow slavery."

(Put down King Clovis) One sad day, King Clovis died. Bathild was very unhappy. She became the only ruler, and again she did not forget the slaves. *(Hold up poor Boy)* She outlawed slavery for all Christians. She had large buildings built all over the country so that men who wanted to become priests and women who wanted to become nuns had places to live.

(Put down poor Boy. Hold up Prince Clotaire. Move Queen to "see" Prince) When Prince Clotaire was only fifteen years old, Bathild went to see him as he practiced using his sword.

"Clotaire, you will now be King of France," Bathild told him. Clotaire was shocked!

"Mother, what do you mean? What do you mean that I am King of France?"

"Clotaire, I am not happy being the Queen. I love God so much, and I want to spend the rest of my life for him. Do you understand?" Clotaire hugged his mother.

"Yes, Mother, I understand. I love God, too, and I know that you will be much happier spending your life for God. But I will miss you!"

(Put down all figures) Bathild said tearful good-byes to all her sons and all her friends in the castle. Then she moved to Chelles, a building where some nuns lived in France. Bathild took nothing that she owned. She was given a very small room, plus one dress and one veil. She was so happy!

For the rest of Bathild's life, she prayed for all her people, including her sons. She also took care of sick people. Finally, Bathild died and went home to God.

Prayer

Dear Saint Bathild, teach me to be obedient, even when I think I'm not being treated fairly. Help me understand that I have to accept some things, like things my parents and teachers tell me. Help me be courageous in doing good things, like stopping kids from making fun of other kids, or telling kids not to say bad words. Thank you for spending your life praying. Teach me to pray, too. Amen.

Words to Know

Kidnap: to be taken away from your home and family by force

Slave: a person who is bought by someone else

Master: someone who has power over another person

Ruler: someone who runs a country, like a king or queen

Rescue: to save someone from something awful

Veil: a piece of fabric worn over a girl or woman's head

Young Bathild

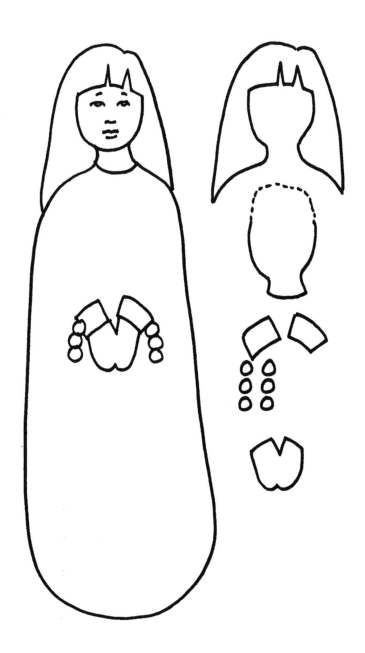

Mary

King Clovis/Prince Clotaire

Queen Bathild

Poor boy

Saint Bernadette

Why This Saint?

Young Bernadette was often ill and, by all accounts, not very smart. However, she did not let her sickness or lack of education affect her goodness, kindness, and obedience. She is a good example for all children to follow.

Lessons to Be Learned

- To realize that God does not always choose the smartest or the healthiest or the best-looking or the most popular people for special missions
- To learn how to obey
- To trust God

Using This Saint

See general instructions that are common to all saints (pp.2-5).

An alternative to *Acting Out the Story* might be to arrange the children in a semi-circle with Bernadette (the catechist) as the day's featured guest speaker. She recounts her visions of the beautiful Lady. She tells the children how she felt about what the Lady told her and what it felt like to be a messenger. Let the children interrupt to ask questions such as, "Why did the Blessed Virgin tell you to wash your face in the mud?"

Then have the children make their own figures of Bernadette and Our Lady to take home with them.

Acting Out the Story

Figures: Young Bernadette, the grotto, Our Lady, Bernadette the nun. Optional: sister and friend (copy Bernadette without water, just hands)

Symbols Mark the Saint

The grotto: The place symbolizes Bernadette's poverty of spirit and down-to-earth approach to life.

The mud and the bitter grass: These were symbols of penance.

Water: A powerful symbol in our Church, representing baptism and the washing away of sin, the living waters with which we are nourished, and the water and the wine in the celebration of the Mass.

Crutches: These are a common symbol for the miracles, especially the many people who have been cured at Lourdes.

If you choose to use the figures to tell the story, here are some suggestions. Either you or the children can make one or more of each of the figures and attach them to popsicle sticks or dowels. Have the children hold their characters up and put them down at the places indicated in the story. Older children might make the characters act out the "actions"; for example, where the characters in the story are walking, have the figures "walk" (move back and forth); when the characters are talking, have the figures face each other and move up and down slightly; and so on.

Story

(Hold up young Bernadette) Bernadette was a very poor little girl who lived in France many years ago. Sometimes she and her family had to go to bed hungry. Bernadette was sick a lot, too. The doctors at that time didn't have all the medicines we have today.

One day, Bernadette was out collecting firewood with her sister and a friend. *(Hold up sister and friend)* The day was chilly. The other girls took off their socks and shoes to walk across the stream. "Come on, Bernadette," her sister shouted. "Would you hurry up? You are such a slow-poke! Look, we're already in the water! Well, we're not waiting for you this time. Stay if you want." And they ran off into the fields.

(Put down sister and friend) Bernadette thought, "Will the cold water make me have another attack of asthma?" But she didn't want to be alone, so she decided to follow anyway.

"I'm coming! I'm hurrying as fast as I can!" she shouted after her companions. But they were already far away. "Oh well, it is true," said Bernadette to herself. "I am a slowpoke. I am not any good at reading, and I can't even write my own name. But that's okay. I am still Bernadette, and Jesus loves me, too!"

(Put down Bernadette) As she sat down to take her socks and shoes off, she heard a loud whooshing sound, like a strong wind. Then she saw something in the nearby cave. *(Hold up grotto)*

(Hold up Bernadette) "What's that? A light? No, it's...what is that?" She tried hard to make it out. "It's a beautiful Lady!" exclaimed Bernadette. *(Hold up Our Lady in "front" of grotto)* The Lady was dressed in white. She wore a blue belt and had a yellow rose on each foot. She held a rosary that was all yellow, just like the roses. She stood above a bush in front of the rock wall. Bernadette was amazed!

(Hold Bernadette facing Our Lady) "The Lady started to say the rosary," Bernadette explained later. She was so happy that she knelt down right away and began to pray the rosary, too. Bernadette never took her eyes off the Lady.

The Lady then motioned for Bernadette to come closer. Bernadette was afraid to go too close to the Lady, and suddenly the Lady just disappeared.

(Put down Bernadette and Our Lady) Later Bernadette saw the beautiful Lady many times. Gradually her parents believed her, and so did many other people. However, the police and the priest and the bishop made it hard for Bernadette and her family.

(Hold up Bernadette and Our Lady) One day the Lady asked Bernadette to do something that seemed silly.

"Bernadette, go drink and wash yourself in the spring," she told her. Bernadette could not find a spring. However, in a corner of the grotto some water was making a little bit of mud. Three times she tried to drink the muddy water and threw it out. Finally, Bernadette took a small amount of water in her hands and drank. Then she washed her face.

"Eat some of that grass, Bernadette." Bernadette obeyed the Lady and ate the grass. When Bernadette turned around, she had grass in her mouth. Her face was covered in mud. All the people laughed at her, but Bernadette still obeyed the Lady.

"Bernadette, you must do penance and pray for sinners," the Lady said over and over again. Bernadette prayed for sinners. Eating the bitter grass was a symbol of penance. So was washing her face in the muddy spring.

"Bernadette," said the Lady, "I want you to tell the priest to build a chapel here for people to come and pray." At first the priest would not even listen to Bernadette. Later, after many tests and many questions, a chapel was built.

(Put down Bernadette and Our Lady) Meanwhile do you know what happened to the small, muddy spring? It became a large spring. When some sick people washed in the water or drank it, they became well. It was a miraculous spring!

Bernadette asked the Lady her name. "I am the Immaculate Conception," said the Lady. Then the people believed that Bernadette saw the Mother of Jesus.

(Hold up Bernadette the nun) Bernadette became a nun. She was a good example to others because of her kindness and obedience. She died when she was thirty-five years old.

The spring is still in the grotto today. Many people are cured of their illnesses there, both physical and spiritual. The Church named Bernadette a saint in 1933. There is now a basilica where Bernadette once kneeled and said the rosary with the beautiful Lady.

Prayer

Dear Saint Bernadette, whether or not I'm really smart doesn't matter. I can still love Jesus. Can you help me be good like you? Help me pray the rosary, too, just as you did. That will make our Blessed Mother happy. Amen.

Words To Know

Rosary: a string of beads we use to pray

Apron: a piece of fabric that you tie around your waist or neck to keep your clothes clean

Penance: an action (good deed or prayer) by which you show God you are sorry for your sins, and also make up for the sins of others

Sinners: people who turn away from God and do things that hurt God and other people

Cured: when you no longer have a sickness

Basilica: a huge church chosen by the pope as a place for receiving special blessings

Messenger: someone who brings news from one person to another or to a group

Young Bernadette/sister, friend

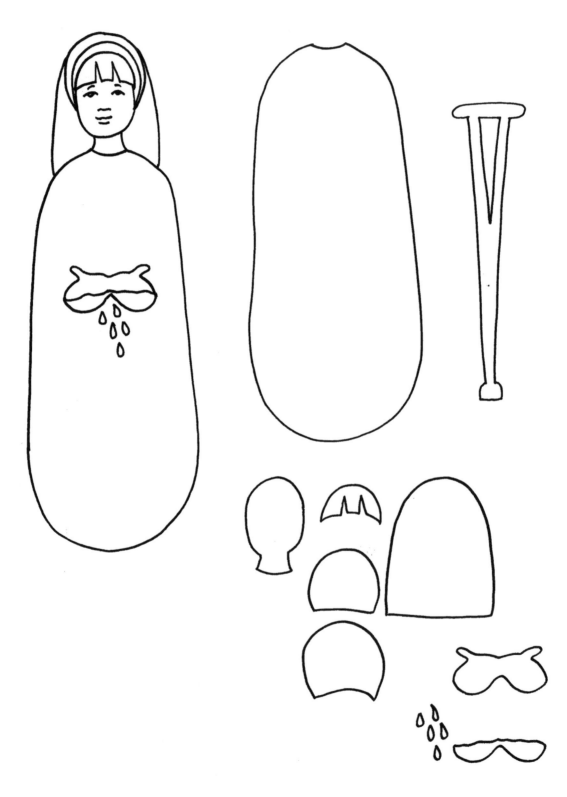

The grotto

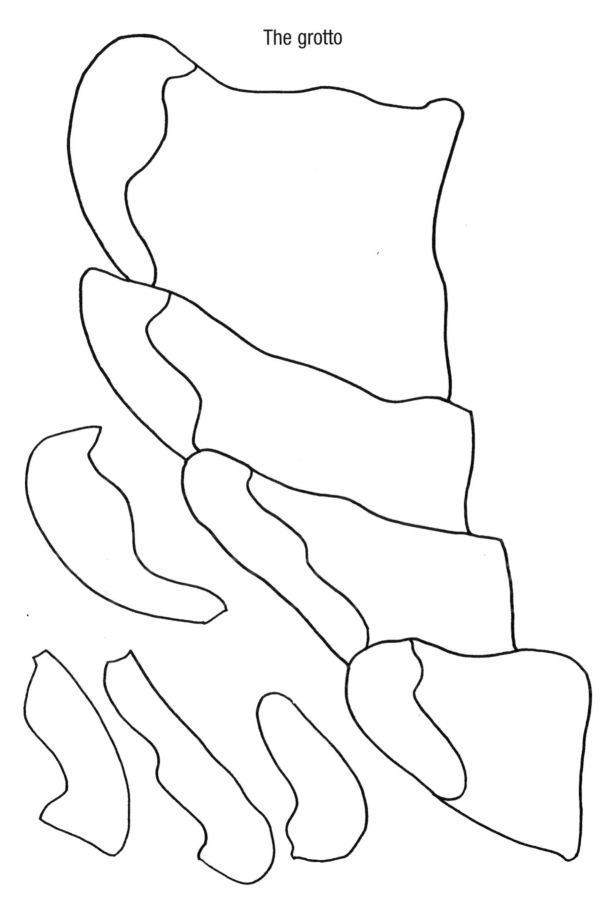

Our Lady

Bernadette the nun

Saint Dominic Savio

Symbols Mark the Saint

Dominic's youth: Age is significant for this saint because a young person can sometimes be seen as less than strong spiritually. However, Dominic's strength surpassed his age.

Why This Saint?

Dominic is an especially fine role model for young boys. He knew when he was very young that he wanted to devote his life to God. He died at age fifteen, having lived a holy life as a child and a teenager.

Dominic's short life was filled with kindness for others and an overwhelming love for God. He was one of ten children. His father was a blacksmith and his mother a seamstress. When Dominic was only five years old, he became an altar boy. When he was twelve, he entered the Oratory School with the intention of becoming a priest. However, he was often sick; he died of illness when he was just fifteen years old.

Lessons to Be Learned

- To recognize that one is never too young to want to spend one's life for God
- To discover another wonderful example of sainthood, Saint John Bosco, Dominic's teacher. Saint John Bosco also wrote Dominic's biography.
- To show that catechists and teachers can influence children in positive ways
- To help children learn to speak up and tell grownups what they want

Using This Saint

See general instructions common to all the saints (pp.2-5).

As an alternative to *Acting Out the Dialogue* make many figures of the children so that your learners can hold impromptu conversations with each other. Suggest themes, such as how to deal with bullying (name-calling, hitting, spitting, punching, etc.) in a Christian way, or attending Mass regularly. If each child is given a Saint Dominic character, perhaps they could make and attach a list of persons they could pray for. The children can place the figure near their beds or bathroom mirrors.

Acting Out the Dialogue

Figures: Dominic, Mother (copy from Saint Maria Goretti, p.101) Father (copy Saint Peter without keys, p.117-118), three other boys (will need to copy one)

If you choose to use the figures for the Dialogue, here are some suggestions. Either you or the children can make one or more of each of the figures and attach them to popsicle sticks or dowels. Have the children hold their characters up and put them down at the places indicated in the story.

Dialogue

Dominic was a young boy when he knew that he loved God very much. When he was only five years old, he became an altar server! Do you know what an altar server is? A server is a child who assists a priest during Mass. Do you remember seeing children helping out? Carrying the water and wine, holding the book the priest reads from?

(Hold up Dominic and Mother)

Dominic   Mother, I want to help the priest during Mass. Can I become an altar server?

Mother   Oh, Dommie, aren't you too little?

Dominic   No, mother, I'm not too little. I love God so much. I will be good. I won't drop the water or the wine or the book. Will you ask father for me?

Mother   Of course. *(Put both figures down)*

Today, there are rules for becoming a server. Children have to wait until they are a little older. If you want to become an altar server when you are older, be sure you tell your mother and father. When he was twelve years old, Dominic wanted to go to school to become a priest.

(Hold up Dominic and Father)

Dominic   Father, I am very proud of who you are and what you do as a blacksmith. But I want to become a priest.

Father   Dominic, you know I always wanted you to take over my business. Yet what better job could there be in the world than loving God! Of course you can go to the Oratory and learn to become a priest.

Dominic   Thank you, Father! I'll go tell Mother! *(Put both figures down)*

Dominic went to the special Oratory School. That's where young boys learned all the important things they needed to know to become priests. Right away, Dominic was well known by all the other boys.

(Hold up Boys)

Boy One   That Dominic, he sure is kind. Do you know he offered to help me with my studies, and he wasn't feeling good at all? He was coughing hard, but he didn't stop helping me. I got an A on my test because of him.

Boy Two   He helped me do the dishes after Mass last night. He wasn't feeling well then either, but he didn't stop. He stayed until every pot and pan was scrubbed clean.

Boy Three	He found me crying in my room a couple of weeks ago. My mother wrote to tell me my dog had died. I was feeling so miserable. Dominic walked by and saw me, so he knocked and came in. He sat beside me and told me that God cared about my dog, too. I felt so much better after that. I mean, I still miss my dog a lot, but Dominic let me know I was not alone. *(Put down Boys)*

Dominic's kindness toward the other boys was noticed by a very special priest at the school, John Bosco. Father Bosco was a teacher there, and he got to know Dominic very well. He told Dominic many things about how to love God and his people. John Bosco is a saint, too. One saint was teaching another saint how to be a saint. Isn't that neat? Now you can learn from Dominic how to be a saint, too.

When Dominic was only fifteen years old, his illness became very bad, and he died. All the boys were so sad! They missed Dominic and his kindness. They knew that he loved God very much. Dominic spoke some special words before he died. He said, "What beautiful things I see!" What do you think he meant?

Dominic Savio was named a saint in 1954.

Prayer

Dear Saint Dominic, I would like to become good, kind, and loving, too. Please help me remember that when I do even little things with love, they are big things in God's eyes. Help me follow your example. Amen.

Words to Know

Altar server: a boy or girl who assists the priest during Mass

Mass: a celebration of Jesus' life, passion, and resurrection

Rules: guides for doing the right thing

Saint: someone who loves God very much and does what pleases God

Dominic

Dominic's friend, boy one

Dominic's friend, boy two

Saint Edith Stein

Why This Saint?

Edith was a great thinker. As a youth, she and her friends discussed philosophy with a passion. This eventually led her to the study of Catholicism. Being baptized a Catholic was quite a choice for her to make because she came from a strong Jewish family. It shows a determination of character that would continue throughout her life.

Young children will not understand the complexities of her thoughts or writings. However, they can understand someone who changes everything in her life to love God more.

The Holocaust is a difficult historical event to present to children. Yet, the admonition at Dachau and the other concentration camps to "Nie Wieder" ("Never Again") suggests that we continue to teach our children the horrors of hatred. Use your discretion in presenting this to the children.

Children are exposed to so much violence in movies and television already. If you are uncomfortable showing the gun that is part of the "props," then don't use it. You don't have to make the characters' facial expressions so mean, either. You can even choose not to use certain characters at all. Pray about it, and take into consideration the age and personalities of your learners. The emphasis should be on learning about the heroism of the saint. Explaining that most of us do not have to experience the suffering of that time is perhaps enough.

Lessons to Be Learned

- To understand that we make thoughtful choices in our lives
- To introduce the Holocaust as a horror born of hatred
- To become sensitive to the beliefs of different people and know that God leads us by various paths

Using This Saint

See general instructions that are common to all saints (pp.2-5).

As an alternative to the Dialogue, you might invite children to become active in helping other children who are "slaves" in one sense or another. Use a map or globe to show the children in which countries children are used for labor in factories, and so on—at least 250 million! See www.freethechildren.com and click on "FTC Worldwide" for information and ideas for activities. Reproduce the image of Edith and let them color her, either as a nun or as a concentration camp prisoner. These can be posted on the map.

Acting Out the Dialogue

Figures: Edith Stein as a young girl (copy Maria Goretti without lilies. p.100), Mother (copy mother from Maria Goretti, p.101), friends (copy young Edith with different hair styles and color clothing), Edith as nun, Edith as prisoner, Soldiers (copy from Saint Maximilian Kolbe, p.113)

If you choose to use the figures for the Dialogue, here are some suggestions. Either you or the children can make one or more of each of the figures and attach them to popsicle sticks or dowels. Have the children hold their characters up and put them down at the places indicated in the story.

Dialogue

When Edith was a little girl, just like you and you and you, she loved to think. She thought about all kinds of things: how things work, what makes people think, who God is.

(Hold up young Edith and Mother)

Edith	Mother, why do birds fly? Why is God love?
Mother	Edith, you ask so many questions! Birds fly because that is how God made them. God is love because he just is. *(Put down young Edith and Mother)*

When Edith grew up, she wanted to know more. She studied with her friends and talked with them.

(Hold up young Edith and Friends)

Edith	Why is God love?
Friend One	I don't know, because God is.
Friend Two	God is love because it took love to make the universe and all of us.
Friend Three	Why do you think God is love, Edith?
Edith	God is love because, even though God is everything, God thinks of others. God cares for his creatures. That's love.
Friend One	That sounds pretty good.
Edith	Do you know anything about Catholicism?
Friend Two	Edith, you're Jewish! Why do you want to know about Catholicism?
Edith	I'm curious about Jesus. If he is God's son, then what a gift, a selfless gift God gave us! I want to know more. *(Put all figures down)*

So she learned more. The more Edith learned, the more she fell in love with Jesus. She also read the life of Saint Teresa of Avila. The saint's story impressed Edith very much.

When Edith was thirty-one years old, she became a Catholic. She was so happy! However, being a Catholic wasn't enough for Edith.

Edith   I want more. I want to love God more and more. I will become a nun!

(Hold up Edith as nun) When Edith was forty-two years old, she became a Carmelite nun and received her new name: Teresa Benedicta of the Cross. Then a terrible war came. It was World War II, and the Jewish people were being hunted like animals. Edith suffered, too, thinking of the suffering of her people.

(Hold up Soldiers) The Nazi soldiers decided that only certain people should be allowed to live. They didn't like Jews, and even though Edith became a Catholic, she was still Jewish by birth. *(Hold up Edith as prisoner)* One day, Edith was taken away from her convent by the soldiers. They took her to a prison camp called Auschwitz. Many Jews were killed there. Edith died there, too, as well as other Catholic priests and nuns.

(Put down all figures)

The Nazi soldiers and their allies lost World War II. Almost all the concentration camps were destroyed. Some of them are left as memorials because the victims and their families don't want anyone to forget what had happened. Six million Jews were killed in World War II. This killing of innocent people is called the Holocaust.

Everyone knew Edith for her loving ways and her prayerful life. Her writings are studied today. She was an intelligent woman, as she'd been a smart little girl. But what we remember Edith for most is her love of God.

The pope named Edith a saint in 1998.

Prayer

Dear Saint Edith, when I am afraid, will you help me? When I am curious about God, will you help me know whom to ask for help? I trust that you will lead me to God, just as you were led to God. Amen.

Words to Know

Catholicism: the belief we share in God the Father, Son, and Holy Spirit, as expressed in the Creed

Selfless: when you think only of others and not yourself

Convent: where nuns live, their home

Nazi soldiers: German soldiers during World War II, who followed Hitler

Concentration camp: a prison camp where people were treated very badly

The Holocaust: the killing of six million Jews and others during World War II

Edith Stein as a nun

Edith Stein as a prisoner

Saint Elizabeth Seton

Why This Saint?

Elizabeth Ann Seton is America's first "daughter" to be canonized a saint. There are four aspects of her example worth noting:

1. Her loving acceptance of God's will.
2. Her love for Jesus in the Eucharist.
3. Her belief in the Blessed Virgin as her own, true Mother.
4. Her devoted work for Catholic education in America.

The thought of embracing our sorrow as it comes from a loving God is a difficult concept for adults to comprehend, let alone practice. We can help children learn how to deal with suffering, setbacks, and pain by presenting the example of this saint's life.

Symbols Mark the Saint

Book: The book symbolizes Elizabeth as a teacher.

Children: They represent Elizabeth's role as mother and as teacher.

Habit: The habit is a sign of Elizabeth's gift of herself to God.

Lessons to Be Learned

- To develop a healthy sense of acceptance of God's will in both the good and the unhappy aspects of our lives
- To compare the way Elizabeth Seton dealt with her sorrows and worries with the way we deal with ours
- To encourage belief that God will help us learn to draw good from bad things that happen
- To grow in our love for Jesus and our Blessed Mother

Using This Saint

See general instructions common for all the saints (pp.2-5).

As an alternative to *Acting Out the Story*, read the Story to the children. Then invite them to make figures of Saint Elizabeth Seton to keep and hang by their bedsides or mirrors to remind them of the lessons they can learn from this saint.

When the figures are completed, the children can use them in other ways.

1. Display them on a bulletin board of your school or religious education program to share with others.

2. Take them to a senior nursing home to display or to give away to the residents.

3. Take them to a retirement home for nuns where children are allowed to meet the residents personally.

Acting Out the Story

Figures: Young Elizabeth (copy young Saint Bathild without chains, p.18), William (copy Saint John Bosco, replace cross and book with buttons and belt, p.77), Our Lady (from Saint Bernadette, p.25), little Girl with book (make a few), Elizabeth as nun

If you choose to use the figures to tell the story, here are some suggestions. Either you or the children can make one or more of each of the figures and attach them to popsicle sticks or dowels. Have the children hold their characters up and put them down at the places indicated in the story. Older children might make the characters act out the "actions"; for example, where the characters in the story are walking, have the figures "walk" (move back and forth); when the characters are talking, have the figures face each other and move up and down slightly; and so on.

Story

(Hold up young Elizabeth) Elizabeth Seton was the daughter of wealthy parents. When Elizabeth was young, her mother died. So she was loved and taken care of by her father, a doctor. Later on Elizabeth's father married again. The stepmother had her own children and treated Elizabeth coldly.

(Hold up William) When Elizabeth was older, she fell in love with a handsome young man, William Seton. He, also, was from a well-to-do family. Elizabeth and William married and had children. Because of their position in society, they went to balls and the theater. *(Move together as if dancing)* They even took part in a ball for President George Washington! It was a wonderful and happy life, just like a fairy tale. *(Put down both figures)*

Then one unhappy thing after another happened. William's father died. Elizabeth and her husband decided to take care of William's younger brothers and sisters, besides their own children. *(Hold up William and Elizabeth)* They tried to keep his family's shipping business going, but it was already in difficulty and soon failed. Now they and their children had little money. William, who had never been very healthy, became very sick. William's doctor suggested a trip to Italy for a change of air, so William and Elizabeth went. However, soon after they reached the home of William's friends, William died. *(Put down William)* What was Elizabeth going to do?

She prayed. "Dear Father in heaven, help me! I am in such need and feel all alone. What can I do to take care of my children?" *(Put down Elizabeth)*

William's friends, the DeFilicchi family, were very kind to her. Elizabeth went to the Catholic church with them, even though she was not Catholic. She felt a strong attraction to Jesus in the Eucharist.

(Hold up Elizabeth and Our Lady) Elizabeth also felt close to Jesus' mother. She began to pray to Mary for help and guidance. "Mary, please be my mother, for I never really had one of my own. Show me how to be a good mother to my children. Ask God to show me his will." *(Put down Our Lady)*

(Move Elizabeth as if crossing ocean) Elizabeth returned to America. She was glad to be home with all her children. Little by little Elizabeth grew to love Jesus and Mary more and more. She became a Catholic. This made most of her family and friends angry.

(Hold up Girls) Elizabeth opened a school for girls in New York to support her family. But not many girls came. Then a priest in Baltimore invited her to open a school there. Elizabeth said to herself, "I am a mother not just for my children, but for all the children I can reach. I will help open Catholic schools for children. They can learn about God and Jesus and Mary our Mother." *(Put down all figures)*

(Hold up Elizabeth as nun) So that is what Elizabeth began to do. She opened the first, free Catholic school in America. Other women joined her, and they all became religious sisters. They opened more schools and two homes for children without parents.

In 1821 Elizabeth died of tuberculosis. She was only forty-six years old. In 1975 she was named a saint—the first American to be honored as a saint!

Prayer

Dear Mother Seton, please help me love Jesus and Mary more and more. Help me have more trust in God when things go wrong in my life. Help me study well, too. Amen.

Words to Know

Business: a way to make a living (for example, as a store owner)

Tuberculosis: a disease that affects the lungs

Young Elizabeth/other girls

Elizabeth as a nun

Saint Faustina

Symbols Mark the Saint

Diary: Sometimes, children are afraid to share their personal thoughts with others out of fear of rejection. The diary symbolizes the validity of personal feelings and thoughts as worthy of God, as well as the obedience Faustina exhibited by writing as Jesus instructed.

Why This Saint?

Faustina Kowalska is one of the many saints recently recognized by the world through the efforts of the late Pope John Paul II. Faustina is considered the secretary of Jesus' message about his divine mercy. Her diary was published as *Divine Mercy in My Soul.* Faustina's humility and obedience in the face of adversity is an admirable quality to teach young children.

In the 1930s, in Poland, Faustina recorded visions and revelations she had. However, since she was basically illiterate, she wrote nearly 700 pages phonetically and without punctuation. Hers is a message of divine love for all humanity. Children need to hear that message, too.

Lessons to Be Learned

- To learn that greatness does not always come in special packages. God loves to show his greatness through persons some might consider lowly.

- To contrast the humble life of Faustina with the greatness of the message Jesus gave directly to her

- To be sensitive to the many ways God speaks to us

- To discover that something as small as a personal diary can become a revelation for the entire world

- To understand what mercy is

- To strengthen our trust in Jesus

Using This Saint

See general instructions common to all the saints (pp.2-5).

As an alternative to *Acting Out the Dialogue,* the children can make little diaries for themselves and use them as a spiritual journal. Staple sheets of lined or plain paper together, with construction paper covers. The children can draw or write their feelings about themselves, their families, God, Jesus, Mary, and their friends. Make Saint Faustina and Jesus figures for each child to glue onto the covers of their books. Invite them to label their diaries with their names, for example, The Diary of Claire or Jake's Diary.

Acting Out the Dialogue

Figures: Jesus, Faustina, frame (if you wish, you might reduce the figure of Jesus and place it within the frame, or make your own frame to the size of the Jesus figure)

If you choose to use the figures for the Dialogue, here are some suggestions. Either you or the children can make one or more of each of the figures and attach them to popsicle sticks or dowels. Have the children hold their characters up and put them down at the places indicated in the story.

Dialogue

(Hold up Jesus and Faustina)

Faustina	Jesus, I love to pray to you. I want to tell you how much I love you.
Jesus	I hear how much you love me, Faustina. I love you, too. I have an important mission for you, my little Faustina. I want you to write down what I am going to tell you. It's all about God's merciful love.
Faustina	But Jesus! I do not know how to write. I only went to school for three years. I am not the person you think I am. I cannot do as you ask.
Jesus	You are the person I want to do this task, Faustina. I know who you are and what you can do. You will be like my secretary. You will write down what I tell you.
Faustina	Jesus, I will obey you and do as you ask. I will get some paper and sew it together to make a little book, a diary. I will write down what you tell me as best I can. *(Put down both figures)*

Jesus told her all about God's mercy. He said that everyone who believes in him can receive this mercy.

(Hold up Jesus and Faustina)

Jesus	Faustina, I want you to spread my message. Tell about the mystery of Divine Mercy to the whole world.
Faustina	Jesus, how can I do this? I am just a nun living quietly in Poland. How can I tell everyone in the world about this beautiful message?
Jesus	You will do this, Faustina. You, too, must trust in me.
Faustina	Yes, Jesus, I trust in you. You will help me bring your message to the world.
Jesus	Now, Faustina, I want you to have a painting made. It will show me just as you see me.
Faustina	But I don't know any artists. I am just a simple nun.
Jesus	You can do this, Faustina. Trust in me.

Faustina   Yes, Jesus. I will go to Mother Superior. I will tell her what you asked.

(Put down both figures) So, Faustina went to her Mother Superior and told her what Jesus had asked of her. Mother Superior brought an artist to the convent. Faustina tried very hard to describe to him what Jesus looked like. Can you imagine how hard that must have been?

Well, when the painting was finished, Faustina didn't like it at all!
(Hold up Jesus, Faustina, and the painting)

Faustina	Jesus, the artist could not paint you as beautiful as you are. I am so upset! You asked me to have the image of you painted as you are. I have failed you.
Jesus	Faustina, you have not failed. It doesn't matter if the painting looks like me or not. What matters is the image. It has been painted well. Do you see the pale light shining from my Sacred Heart? That stands for the waters of baptism. The pale red light is the blood of my sacrifice. Through these everyone shall receive my Divine Mercy. The words, "Jesus, I trust in you," will be translated into every language.
Faustina	Jesus, I am so glad you are happy. I still don't understand how all this will come to be. But I do trust in you. I love you so much.
Jesus	Faustina, I love you, too. *(Put down all the figures)*

So, Faustina wrote in her diary and now you can read it. It has been published all over the world. Just as Jesus said, the words on the painting have been translated into many languages. Everyone can hear the message Jesus gave through Faustina: that God offers us his Divine Mercy.

Prayer

Dear Saint Faustina, you didn't think you could do what Jesus asked, but you still tried. When Jesus asked you for something, you didn't understand how it would happen but you still trusted him. Help me trust Jesus as much as you do, Saint Faustina. Amen.

Words to Know

Diary: a little book where you write your feelings or thoughts

Artist: someone who creates beautiful things, like paintings and drawings and statues

Fail: to be unable to complete a task

Trust: to believe with your whole heart

Mercy: great loving kindness

Publish: to make lots of copies of a book to sell

Translate: to put the words in one language into different languages

Faustina

Jesus/frame

Jesus,
I trust in you.

Saint Hildegard von Bingen

Symbols Mark the Saint

Quill and Book: These represent Hildegard's writings in which she recorded her many visions, as well as her musical compositions.

Music Note: This is a contemporary symbol, not part of her actual symbolic history. It emphasizes the musical aspects of her life.

Why This Saint?

Hildegard was a medieval visionary, a musician, a poet, a mystic, and an anchoress or hermit. She is revered for her strength, creativity, and openness to the expression of God's personal gifts of revelation. Her relevance for children is multi-faceted. She offered praise to God through her musical compositions. These pieces are still played and enjoyed today. They remind children that God loves to hear from us through different creative means, giving glory to God through our gifts.

Lessons to Be Learned

- To realize that making music through singing, playing an instrument, humming, dancing, is a beautiful and wonderfully expressive way to show God how much we love him

- To understand that God is an infinitely creative being. Our creativity pleases God when we use the gifts God gave us to praise him.

- To experience music together and know that we can enjoy it by ourselves and with others

Using This Saint

See general instructions common for all the saints (pp.2-5).

Here are some alternatives to *Acting Out the Story*.

1. Talk to the children about this saint, who is not officially canonized but is beatified and commonly recognized as a saint. You can even sing about her. For example, sing the following to "All around the Mulberry Bush" or another tune the words fit to: "Hildegard wrote beautiful music to show God how much she loves him." You could take a sentence from the story and set it to music. The point is to be spontaneous and free from critique.

2. Use instruments like bells, sticks, or even kazoos to loosen the children up and let them experience music with God in mind. Remember to smile, applaud, and encourage every child with lots of compliments.

3. Make and use the figures as the children sing familiar songs. Have them move the figures around to animate their music.

Acting Out the Story

Figures: Young Hildegard singing, young Hildegard, Hildegard as an anchoress, Jutta the anchoress

If you choose to use the figures to tell the story, here are some suggestions. Either you or the children can make one or more of each of the figures and attach them to popsicle sticks or dowels. Have the children hold their characters up and put them down at the places indicated in the story. Older children might make the characters act out the "actions"; for example, where the characters in the story are walking, have the figures "walk" (move back and forth); when the characters are talking, have the figures face each other and move up and down slightly; and so on.

Story

Do you ever make up songs? Maybe your mom or dad sing to you at bedtime. When you are in church do you sing with all the people? Those songs are written by lots of different people. They are beautiful songs. Did you know that God loves it when you make up songs just for him? Did you know that a song can be a gift?

(Hold up young Hildegard singing) Well, Hildegard von Bingen wrote songs. She has a long name, doesn't she? Do you know anyone named Hildegard? Do you know how to say her name? You say it, Hill–da–guard. And von means from. So, Hildegard is from Bingen, a city in Germany. *(Put down Hildegard)*

Say your name, then say von, then say the city or town you live in. For example: Marie lives in Chicago, so she would be Marie von Chicago. Other examples are Ian von Cleveland, or Christian von New York. That's a neat way to say who you are, don't you think?

(Hold up young Hildegard, not singing) Hildegard lived almost 1,000 years ago. She was born in 1098. She lived a long time, too. She was eighty-one years old when she died.

Life was very different then from now. When Hildegard was only eight years old, she was sent away from home to live with a woman named Jutta. *(Hold up Jutta)* Jutta was her teacher. She especially taught Hildegard how to live more like Jesus.

Jutta said to Hildegard, "I am an anchoress. Do you know what that means, child?"

"No," said Hildegard. "I know that my parents brought me here to be your pupil."

"Well," said Jutta, "an anchoress is a woman who lives in a tiny room right next to the church in the town. We only have a small window to see the world. Kind people will bring us food, which we can share." *(Put down Hildegard and Jutta)*

What did an anchoress do all day? She would pray a lot, sew to mend clothes, or make pretty things with colored thread. The idea was to not be a part of the world, to live only for God.

(Hold up Hildegard as anchoress) Later Hildegard also lived this way, all by herself. She offered up her life a gift to God. She thought only of him and others her whole life.

Hildegard also had a special gift. She made beautiful music and musical plays. She wrote them as a gift to God and to bring other people to God. The people loved to sing and perform in them. *(Put down Hildegard)*

Her music is almost 1,000 years old! Do you know what? Her music is still being sung today. Many people love to play her music. Hildegard's gift for God is still a gift for God today! Isn't that neat?

Prayer

Dear Saint Hildegard, you made beautiful music for God. You thought all the time of making him happy and making him smile. Let me make beautiful music, too! I will sing a happy song to God when I am happy and a sad song to God when I am sad. I can share my song with my mom and dad, sisters and brothers, and teacher and friends. When I share gifts, I make God happy. Amen.

Words to Know

Music: putting sounds together to make a beautiful work

One thousand: equal to 100 times ten

Religion: learning about God and Jesus and the Church

Anchoress: a woman who gives up everything for God and lives alone (a man is called an anchorite)

Mend: to sew torn clothes or socks

Gift: something you give to someone else with love in your heart

Musical: telling a story by using dialogue, actions, and songs

Composition: writing a song to sing or to play with an instrument

Young Hildegard singing

Young Hildegard

Hildegard as an anchoress

Jutta the anchoress

Young Anthony, p.10

Father, p.11

Mother, p.12

Anthony the priest, p.13

Young Bathild, p.18

Mary, p.19

King Clovis / Prince Clotair, p.20

Queen Bathild, p.21

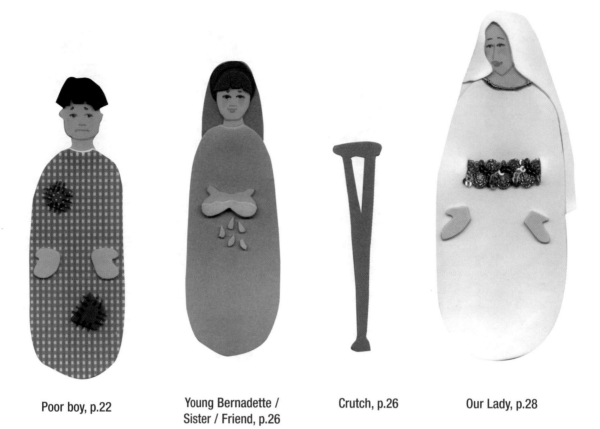

Poor boy, p.22

Young Bernadette /
Sister / Friend, p.26

Crutch, p.26

Our Lady, p.28

Grotto, p.27

Bernadette the nun, p.29

Dominic, p.33

Dominic's friend, boy one, p.34

Dominic's friend / boy two p.35

Edith Stein as a nun, p.39

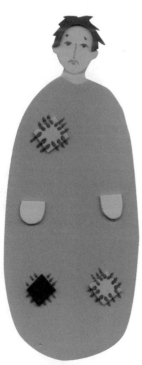

Saint Edith Stein as a prisoner, p.40

Young Elizabeth Seton / other girl, p.44

Elizabeth Seton as a nun, p.45

Faustina, p.49

Jesus for frame, pp.50,51

Singing girl, p.55

Young Hildegard, p.56

Hildegard as an anchoress, p.57

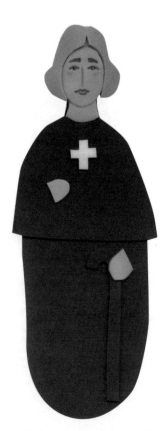

Jutta the anchoress, p.58

Young Joan, p.70

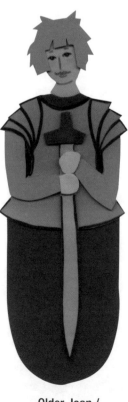

Older Joan /
Joan as a soldier, p.71

Dauphin, p.72

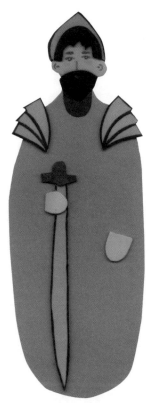

Soldier, p.73

John Bosco as a priest, p.77

Juan Diego without roses, p.81

Our Lady of Guadalupe, p.82

The Bishop, p.83

Juan Diego with roses and a figure of Our Lady, p.84

Blessed Kateri, p.88

Aunt, p.89

Missionary, p.90

Katharine as a nun, p.94

Native American Girl, p.95

African American Girl, p.96

Maria, p.100

Mother, p.101

Alessandro, p.102

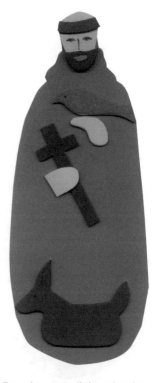

Francis as a religious brother, p.106

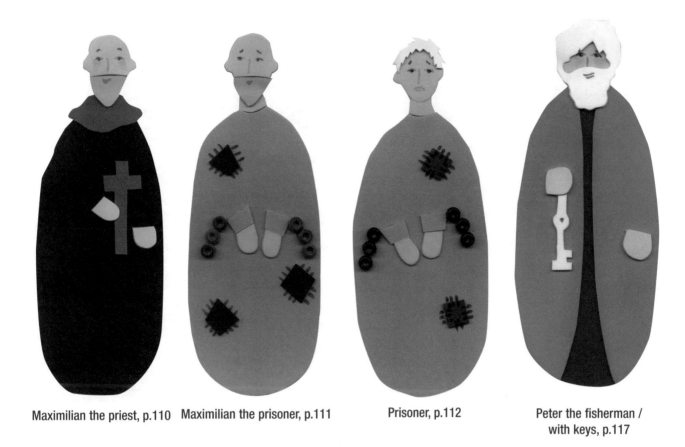

Maximilian the priest, p.110   Maximilian the prisoner, p.111   Prisoner, p.112   Peter the fisherman / with keys, p.117

Boat, p.119   Jesus, p.120   Mother Teresa, p.124

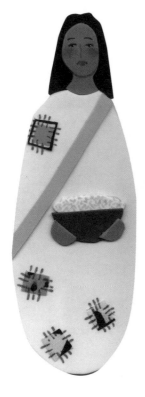

Buhkti, p.125

Young Thérèse, p.129

Thérèse's Father, p.130

Thérèse as a nun, p.131

Abraham, p.135

Sarah (with baby Isaac), p.136

Angel, p.137

Issac, p.138

Saint Joan of Arc

Why This Saint?

Joan has been a particular favorite of young children throughout the years. As a young girl, she was called to acts of great heroism. To realize that a young teen—a girl at that—led the French army is a fascinating story in itself.

But Joan's life and death have great meaning for children. She did not become a saint because she led an army. Her prayer life, her obedience to God, taking on an impossible task and sticking to her intent despite mortal threats, are all the qualities of a holy life.

Lessons to Be Learned

- To develop a personal relationship with God through prayer and listening. God speaks in different ways.

- To obey God and parents. Not everyone is called to heroic deeds, but seeing Joan accept and follow God's will in such a self-sacrificing way can inspire children to obey in small and big things.

- To trust parents when they ask children to do something, like picking up their toys, sitting still in church or a doctor's office, or tasting a food they think they might dislike

- To refrain from teasing or taunting others and instead be kind as Saint Joan was

Using This Saint

See general instructions common to all the saints (pp.2-5).

Acting Out the Story

Figures: Young Joan, older Joan (use soldier Joan without armor), Joan as soldier, Dauphin, soldier (make more than one soldier to complete the army)

If you choose to use the figures to tell the story, here are some suggestions. Either you or the children can make one or more of each of the figures and attach them to popsicle sticks or dowels.

Symbols Mark the Saint

Armor: Armor represents warfare but it also symbolizes Joan's strength of character and commitment to God.

Sword: Certainly a symbol of the real threat of death, it emphasizes that Joan fought for God.

Cut hair: In Joan's day, women wore long hair. By cutting her hair, she showed how serious she was in her allegiance to God.

Have the children hold their characters up and put them down at the places indicated in the story. Older children might make the characters act out the "actions"; for example, where the characters in the story are walking, have the figures "walk" (move back and forth); when the characters are talking, have the figures face each other and move up and down slightly; and so on.

Story

Joan of Arc. You might think that Joan's last name is Arc. Instead Arc means that Joan was from the town of Arc in France, a big country in Europe. She lived in the early 1400s, which is almost 600 hundred years ago! It was a different time, a time of kings and castles.

(Hold up young Joan) Joan had four siblings, that is, brothers and sisters. Her parents were named Jacques and Isabelle. When Joan was a little girl, her job was to watch the sheep.

Then, when Joan was thirteen, she began to hear voices of saints and angels. She also saw figures in light. These are called visions. The voices told her she had a mission: to save France. "Go, daughter of God!" they urged her. *(Put down young Joan)*

Joan had a hard time convincing the French commander in their area, but he finally sent her to the Dauphin. The Dauphin was supposed to be the King of France.

(Hold up older Joan and the Dauphin) Joan said to the Dauphin Charles, "Your father was King of France, but now the English are the rulers of our country. You are supposed to be the king. I will put you on the throne."

Charles said, "Joan, you are just a girl! How are you supposed to make me the King of France?"

"I will become a soldier and lead the army!" she cried.

Charles was surprised. "You, lead an army? How? You are just a girl!"

"I will wear armor," she said. "And I will ride a horse, carry a sword, and lead the men into battle. I will die, if I have to."

Charles believed she could do this wonderful miracle. He said, "Yes, Joan. I am supposed to be the King of France. I will give you the armies you need to take France away from the English and give it back to our people." *(Put down Joan and Dauphin)*

(Hold up Joan as soldier, plus other Soldiers) Joan did what she promised. She fought together with the French soldiers. Do you think they would listen to a girl? At first it was hard to convince some of them. At last, when they realized God had really sent her, they did listen. Joan would tell the men what God wanted them to do.

"Soldiers of France! Today is a great day," Joan yelled across the fields to hundreds of soldiers. "We will fight today, we will fight to free France. We will fight to have a French King. We will fight for what is right. We will fight for God's will!" All the soldiers cheered!

"Joan! We will follow you into battle. We fight for France. We will fight for God!" They fought right beside Joan. Sometimes the soldiers got hurt, including Joan. And sometimes they died. But most often they won. *(Put down soldiers one by one)*

(Hold up Dauphin with Joan) After one big battle, Joan came to Charles and said, "We have led many troops to victory. Now you can be crowned King in the city of Orleans." So Charles was crowned King of France. *(Put down Dauphin and Joan)*

Then a terrible thing happened. Joan's enemies, the English, captured her. She was in a lot of trouble. They didn't like the fact that she had won in battle and that Charles was king.

(Hold up Joan, without armor) Her enemies accused her of heresy because she believed in her voices. Some said she was a witch. They put Joan in prison. She was put on trial to decide if she was innocent or guilty. Joan was very brave. She answered all of their questions honestly.

"I obeyed God," she said.

Her enemies said, "You're guilty of heresy. The penalty is death. You, Joan of Arc, will die!" *(Put down Joan)*

In May of 1432, when Joan was only nineteen years old, she was declared guilty of heresy and witchcraft. She was tied to a big, wooden pole in the middle of town. Sticks were placed all around her feet and then they were put on fire. Joan died.

In 1920, the Church cleared her name and declared her a saint. Many people still honor and pray to her today, 600 years later. Saint Joan of Arc is known for her courage in speaking God's word, even when she suffered for it.

Prayer

Dear Saint Joan, sometimes people may make fun of me or say things about me that aren't true. Then let me think of you. Sometimes I may tell people that I love Jesus. If they laugh at me, let me think of you. When I am afraid to tell the truth, let me think of you. Help me be strong like you. Amen.

Words to Know

Victory: winning, especially winning a game or battle

Trial: a court of law to decide if a person is innocent or guilty

Vision: to see or hear something others might not; usually a religious experience

Innocent: when a person has not committed the act they are accused of

Dauphin: a man who is next in line to be king

Guilty: when a person does something wrong

Armor: metal suit that protected soldiers in battle

Young Joan

Older Joan/Joan as a soldier

Dauphin

Soldier

Saint John Bosco

Why This Saint?

John Bosco loved children. His influence extended into the life of little Dominic Savio. John Bosco was his teacher and his mentor. Both are saints. This says something about this particular saint's life.

His methods were a little unorthodox. His dreams played a pivotal role in the direction of his mission. He took in hundreds of unwanted boys, and opened refuges for them. He taught them skills such as shoemaking, printing, and carpentry. Through love and gentleness, Father John helped them change their lives and brought them to God.

Lessons to Be Learned

- To expand awareness of God's voice, even through dreams
- To show that God speaks in many ways
- To talk about how to listen to God's voice
- To introduce humility, faithfulness, and strength as a way to effect positive change in others

Using This Saint

See general instructions common to all saints (pp.2-5).

Acting Out the Story

Figures: young John Bosco (copy Dominic Savio, change hair, p.33), John Bosco the priest, Boys, one of whom is Petey (copy or use the boys from Dominic Savio, pp.34,35)

A gold cord can be used for the chain around the saint's neck. An adult can use hot glue to put a spot in the front and on the two ends in the back.

If you choose to use the figures to tell the story, here are some suggestions. Either you or the children can make one or more of each of the figures and attach them to popsicle sticks or dowels. Have the children hold their characters up and put them down at the places indicated in the story.

Older children might make the characters act out the "actions"; for example, where the characters in the story are walking, have the figures "walk" (move back and forth); when the characters are talking, have the figures face each other and move up and down slightly; and so on.

Story

(Hold up young John) When John Bosco was nine years old, he had a very special dream. He dreamed that he was standing in a field with a lot of other children. But the children were being very naughty. They were swearing and fighting and doing all kinds of naughty things. John only wanted to stop them, so he stepped into the crowd of kids. He began yelling at them to stop.

Suddenly, a man wearing all white appeared. He called John over to him and said, "You are now the leader of this gang of boys."

The man continued telling John what he was to do. "You need to make friends with these boys," the man said. "To be friends, you have to be kind and gentle. You see, John, this will be your mission in life." *(Put down John)*

John woke up and told his family about the dream. In his heart, he believed it meant that he was to become a priest and help children.

(Hold up John as priest) John did become a priest. He went into the streets where the boys were often fighting. He did just what the man in the dream had told him. *(Hold up Boys)* He was gentle and kind to the boys. They responded by being kind and gentle, too. John learned how to do magic tricks and juggle. Then the boys would pay attention to him. After, he'd take them to Mass.

He set up workshops. There the boys learned how to be shoemakers, printers, and carpenters. They learned about God's love for them. Gradually they would change. They stopped being naughty boys and grew up to be fine men. *(Put down John and Boys)*

Other men joined him. Together they became the community known as the Salesian priests and brothers.

(Hold up John as priest and Petey) One day one of the boys, named Petey, came to see him. "Father Bosco, why didn't you punish me when I stole the candle from the church?" asked Petey. Petey often had nothing to eat. He hoped to sell the candle for a piece of bread.

"Petey," answered John Bosco, "did you know stealing the candle was wrong?"

"Yes, Father, I know it was wrong, but I was hungry," Petey said, his eyes filling up with tears.

"Okay, Petey," said John Bosco, "let's go into the church. You can ask Jesus to forgive you. Then we'll go into the house and get you some nice hot soup and a big piece of bread. How does that sound?"

"You are going to give me food because I stole a candle?" Petey still couldn't believe what was happening.

"I'm giving you food because I love you, and God loves you, and you are hungry, Petey. Isn't that enough?"

"I guess so," said Petey, but he still wasn't sure. "Why do you love me? Why does God love me?" Petey asked.

"God loves you, Petey, because you are a good boy inside! Stealing and fighting and swearing are all things you can stop doing. But God will never stop loving you, no matter what you do. Now, can't you love God a little? And if you love him, you don't want to hurt him, do you?"

"Oh no, Father John! I don't want to hurt God!" said Petey, wiping his tears with the back of his hand.

"Then let's practice not swearing because that hurts God. And let's practice not fighting because that hurts God. And let's practice not stealing because..." but John Bosco didn't have a chance to finish.

"Because that hurts God," Petey finished, "and I don't want to hurt God ever again!"

"See, Petey, you are a good boy!" said John Bosco with a bigger smile and a bigger hug as he took Petey to the kitchen for that soup and bread. *(Put down John and Petey)*

A dream put John Bosco on the path of helping little boys learn skills as well as goodness. He was a very good man. The Church named him a saint in 1934.

Prayer

Dear Saint John Bosco, sometimes other children yell at me or hit me or call me names. I want to yell or hit back. Help me, instead, to be patient and to love them the way you did, the way Jesus does. Amen.

Words to Know

Dream: a story that happens in your mind when you sleep

Swearing: saying bad words that offend God

Impossible: when something cannot be done

Pay attention: to look at someone or listen to someone carefully

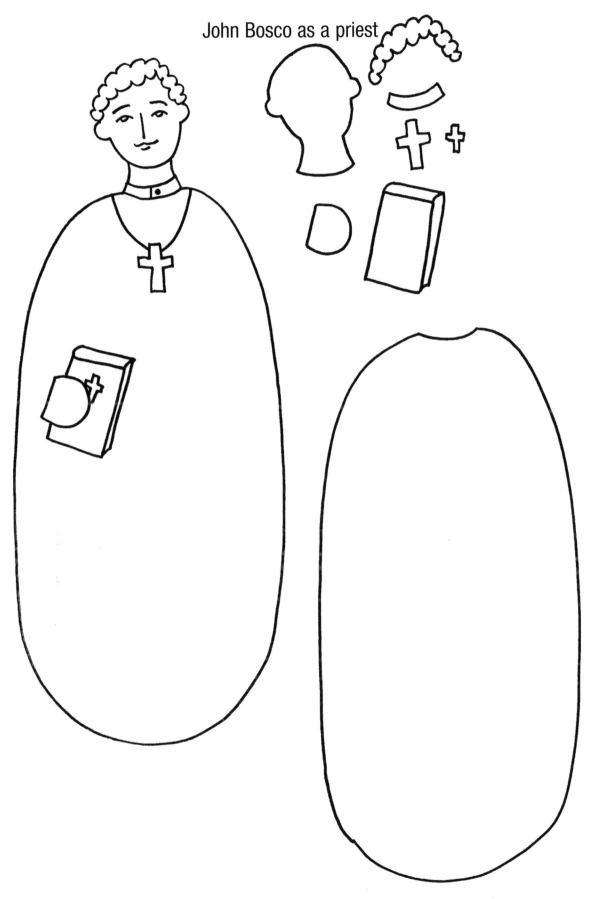

John Bosco as a priest

Saint Juan Diego

Symbols Mark the Saint

Tilma: Juan Diego's tilma hangs in the Basilica of Our Lady of Guadalupe in Mexico City. The tilma is considered a great mystery and miracle.

Roses: These flowers, which bloomed out of season, represent Mary's loving response to Juan's faith.

Why This Saint?

Our Blessed Mother set the tone for this saint by calling him her little Juanito and declaring herself his mother. What child would not feel drawn to such a tender mother?

Juan's reluctance to obey Mary is also something children can relate to. That Mary surprised him on the road when he chose to avoid her would tickle most children!

Lessons to Be Learned

• To explore what it means to have a special experience, like seeing the Blessed Virgin Mary

• To learn that Mary is our mother and loves us as our mothers do

• To witness the power of a miracle and its impact on people 500 years later

• To recognize that the Catholic Church is universal

Using This Saint

See general instructions common to all the saints (pp.2-5).

Acting Out the Story

Figures: Juan Diego without roses, Our Lady of Guadalupe, the bishop, Juan Diego with roses, Juan Diego with roses and the figure of Our Lady. For Juan's tilma, you can use ribbon roses purchased at a craft store instead of the foam circles. You can also make a tilma out of burlap and actually place it over the figure.

Included is a picture of Our Lady of Guadalupe you can trace or photocopy, then glue onto the front of Juan Diego's tilma before he appears before the bishop for the last time.

If you choose to use the figures to tell the story, here are some suggestions. Either you or the children can make one or more of each of the figures and attach them to popsicle sticks or dowels. Have the children hold their characters up and put them down at the places indicated in the story. Older children might make the characters act out the "actions"; for example, where the characters in the story are walking, have the figures "walk" (move back and forth); when the characters are talking, have the figures face each other and move up and down slightly; and so on.

Story

(Hold up Juan Diego without roses) Juan Diego was a very poor man who lived near Mexico City, a big city in Mexico. He lived a long time ago, in 1474, even before Columbus arrived in America! Every day, Juan Diego got up before the sun rose and walked fifteen miles to Mexico City to attend Mass. One day, while he was in the mountains, he heard beautiful music and a voice calling him.

(Hold up Our Lady) "Juanito, the littlest of my sons, where are you going?" *Juanito* means "my little Juan." It expresses great love. Juan was surprised to see a beautiful lady standing there.

"I am the Blessed Virgin," she told him. "Juanito, I want a church to be built right here so my love, compassion, help, and defense can be felt. I am your most devoted mother. Go tell all this to the bishop." *(Put down Our Lady)*

(Juan "goes to bishop." Hold up the Bishop) Juan Diego went right away to the bishop to tell him of Our Lady's desire.

"What do you want, Juan Diego?" asked the bishop.

"I have seen the Blessed Virgin. She asks that a church be built on Tepeyac Hill. She wants to show her love for us, her people."

The bishop didn't believe Juan Diego. He said, "Juan, I need some proof that this lady you say you saw is truly the Blessed Virgin." *(Put down the Bishop)*

(Juan "goes back") Juan Diego was going right away to see the Lady to tell her. Then he got a message that his uncle was dying. "Uncle is dying! He needs a priest. If I go up the mountain, the Lady will be there. My poor uncle may die all alone. I will go another way so I won't be late for my uncle."

Can you guess what happened? Our Lady appeared to him on the other road he took.

(Hold up Our Lady) "Where are you going, Juanito?" she asked him, although she already knew the answer.

"My Lady, I know I am making you unhappy. But my uncle is dying, and I am hurrying to get the priest. When I'm finished, I'll come back to see you."

Our Lady surprised him with her answer. "Listen to me, my little Juan. Don't be afraid or sad. Your uncle will not die now. He is already cured."

"My Lady, let me take proof to the bishop that you are who you say you are."

"Climb the mountain, Juanito," the Lady said. "On the spot where you first saw me, you will find beautiful flowers blooming. Cut them, gather them, and put them together in a bouquet. Then come and bring them to me."

(Put down Our Lady. Juan "climbs mountain") Immediately Juan Diego climbed to the top of the mountain. All sorts of beautiful roses growing everywhere the Lady had been! And do you

know what? This was in the month of December! It was too cold for flowers to bloom. What a great miracle! *(Put down Juan without roses)*

Juan cut the roses, gathered them together, and put them into his tilma. *(Hold up Juan with roses)* Then he brought them to Our Lady.

(Hold up Our Lady) Our Lady said, "Juanito, here is proof for the bishop. Now you are to open your tilma only in front of him. Tell him I wish that a church be built here, just as I have asked." *(Put down Our Lady and Juan)*

When Juan reached the bishop's house, no one would let him in! He waited a very long time outside. Finally, Juan Diego was let inside the bishop's house.

(Hold up Bishop) When Juan stood in front of the bishop, he opened his tilma. *(Hold up Juan with roses and figure of Our Lady)* All the roses fell onto the floor. Then do you know what happened? A picture of Our Lady appeared on the front of Juan Diego's tilma! She looked exactly as Juan Diego had seen her. The bishop was amazed and fell to his knees.

"Please forgive me, my Lady, for not believing you and not obeying you right away!" the bishop cried. *(Put down all figures)*

Now in Mexico City, there is a huge church—a basilica—called Our Lady of Guadalupe. Every year, hundreds of thousands of people go there to pray to Mary. Juan Diego's tilma is hanging in the Basilica so everyone can see it. Even though it is more than 500 years old, it looks just as it did on the day he opened it for the bishop.

The pope named Juan Diego a saint on July 31, 2002.

Prayer

Dear Saint Juan Diego, help me remember that Our Lady loves me very much, just as she loved you. When I feel sad, help me remember the miracle of the roses. I will do all my little tasks with love. I will love Our Lady, just as you do. Amen.

Words to Know

Tilma: a poncho-like apron that covers a person in front and back

Devoted: when you love something and take care of it

Protect: to try not to let anything bad happen to something or someone you care about

Disturbed: when you are upset about something

Proof: when you can show that something is true

Fragrance: a wonderful smell

Obey: to listen and do what people who love you, including God, tell you to

Basilica: a huge church in which people can receive special blessings

Juan Diego without roses

Our Lady of Guadalupe

The bishop

Juan Diego with roses and a figure of Our Lady

Blessed Kateri Tekakwitha

Why This Saint?

Kateri Tekakwitha is the first Native American to be declared blessed. America's spiritual progress includes the celebration of all nationalities. Encouraging prayer to and imitation of this young woman is a marvelous way to reinforce "one nation under God." Also, her facial disfigurement caused by smallpox can be helpful to children who are bullied for any reason. As the patroness of the environment and ecology, she joins Saint Francis of Assisi in love and protection of God's creation.

Lessons to Be Learned

- To understand that people with disabilities are capable of great spiritual achievements
- To be proud of who we are and to know we are the well-loved children of God
- To understand how belief in Jesus is greater than anything else we can learn
- To introduce the idea of penance, and that God can bring good out of suffering
- To inspire devotion to the Holy Eucharist

Using This Saint

See general instructions common to all the saints (pp.2-5).

As an alternative to *Acting Out the Story*, help the children do research on Kateri, in the library and on the internet. Search on the web for "Kateri Tekakwitha" and you will find several sites, including that of her national shrine. At http://conservation.catholic.org/kateri, for example, you will find the oldest portrait of Blessed Kateri (@1680's).

Acting Out the Story

Figures: Blessed Kateri, aunts (make two), missionary

You can make a fringe on Kateri's dress by cutting a narrow strip of paper or foam, then cut-

Symbols Mark the Saint

Native American dress: The dress is a symbol that we are united in God's love and as brothers and sisters, while we each celebrate our individual and unique heritage.

The cross: This symbol expresses Kateri's love for Jesus crucified and her faithfulness to the Mass.

ting little slits the full length. An adult can hot glue beads on. You can also cut out and glue shapes of animals or trees on the dress to signify Native American symbols.

If you choose to use the figures to tell the story, here are some suggestions. Either you or the children can make one or more of each of the figures and attach them to popsicle sticks or dowels. Have the children hold their characters up and put them down at the places indicated in the story. Older children might make the characters act out the "actions"; for example, where the characters in the story are walking, have the figures "walk" (move back and forth); when the characters are talking, have the figures face each other and move up and down slightly; and so on.

Story

Kateri Tekakwitha. What an unusual name! Can you say it all together with me? Do you know what kind of name that is? It's Native American. Sometimes we call Native Americans "Indians," but the correct term is Native American.

Kateri was born right here in the United States, in New York, in 1656. Her mother was an Algonquin and a Christian. She taught little Kateri about Jesus. Kateri's father was a Mohawk chief.

When Kateri was four years old, her family died of a terrible disease called smallpox. Smallpox covers your body with sores, kind of like chicken pox, but much worse. They leave a lot of scars.

(Hold up Kateri) Kateri caught smallpox, too, but she didn't die. However, the sores left her with scars all over her beautiful face. It was all bumpy and lumpy, and she was rather ugly.

(Hold up aunts) Kateri had two aunts and an uncle who adopted Kateri and brought her to live with them. "I miss my family," Kateri told her aunts and uncle. Her uncle was very good to her. The aunts did not like her and thought she was lazy.

"Your family is with the earth," they told her. They did not believe in Jesus. *(Put down all figures)*

Kateri grew up into a kind and good young woman. When she was twenty years old, missionaries came to her village. They traveled around the country teaching people who Jesus is.

(Hold up Kateri and missionaries) "Kateri, we are missionaries," they said. "We want to tell you about Jesus because he loves you so much."

"My mother taught me about Jesus when I was little," Kateri said. "But I would like to know more." *(Put down all figures)*

The missionaries told her all about him. They taught her how he was born and lived and died for all of us. They told Kateri that Jesus loved her and all her people.

(Hold up Kateri and aunts) "I am beginning to love Jesus," she told her aunts and uncle. They were very angry.

"Kateri, you are a Mohawk. You must believe in the ways of our people."

"But now I know Jesus better," Kateri told them, "I will still do all my chores and try to be an obedient daughter. But I can't practice your way any more." *(Put down all figures)*

Kateri was baptized in 1676. The priests worried for Kateri's safety. So they secretly helped her go to Canada. A group of Christians already had a home there. Kateri was able to freely live her belief in Jesus.

(Hold up Kateri and missionary) "I love the Mass," she said to one of the priests.

"Yes, Kateri, I know you do. I see you standing outside the chapel door every single morning. You will get sick standing out there in the cold winter air." *(Put down missionary)*

Kateri loved to participate at Mass. Most of all, she loved to receive the Eucharist, the body and blood of Jesus. She knew Jesus had died for all of us. She prayed that her people would come to know Jesus. *(Put down Kateri)*

Kateri died when she was only twenty-four years old. But her work didn't stop. People had watched how she prayed and made sacrifices. They saw how kind she was to others. Their curiosity about Jesus led them to the missionaries who taught them about Jesus and the Church, too.

Kateri was a Native American and her people respect the earth and want to take care of it. So Kateri was named the patroness of the environment and ecology along with Saint Francis of Assisi. We need to respect and care for the gifts of the earth that God has given us.

In 1980, Kateri was beatified by the pope. She has not yet been named a saint, but someday she will be.

Prayer

Dear Blessed Kateri, you were strong in your belief in Jesus even when no one else around you believed. You loved others so much that you wanted them to know Jesus, too. Help me believe and act as you did out of love for Jesus. I will remember to take care of the earth, too. I will not waste water or litter or do things that damage it. God gave us the earth for our home. Amen.

Words To Know

Native Americans: the first people to live in the Americas

Scar: a mark that remains on your skin after you have a sore or a wound

Missionaries: people who travel around the world to teach others about Jesus

Patroness: a woman saint chosen because of her care for something or because of a particular event or characteristic of her life

Environment: the place where you live, like the earth, the country, the neighborhood

Ecology: the science where people study the connection between living things and their environment

Beatify: to declare that someone who has died is in heaven

Blessed Kateri

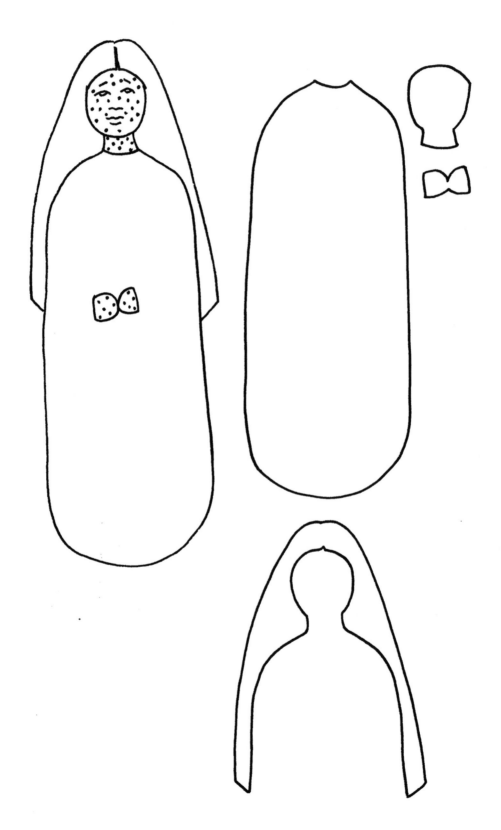

Aunt

Missionary

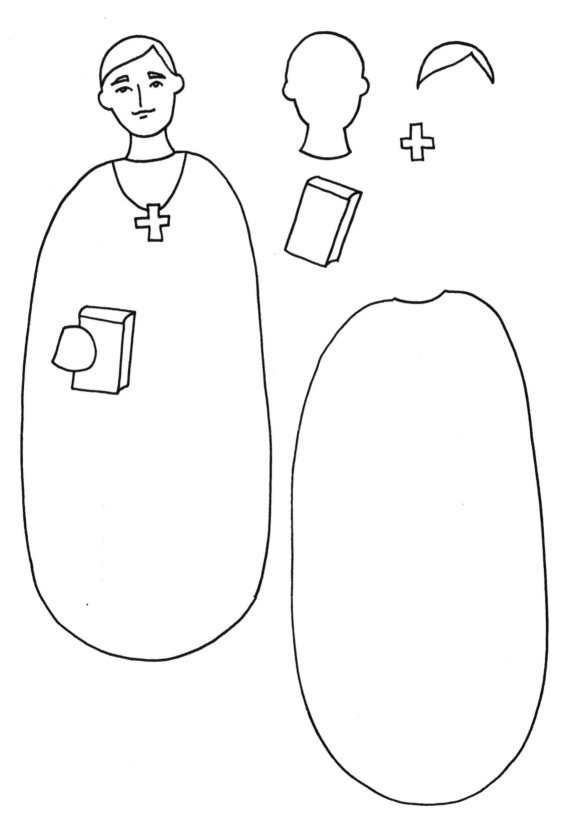

Saint Katharine Drexel

Why This Saint?

Katharine was the daughter of a wealthy family in Philadelphia. She used her riches to care for Native Americans, African Americans, and the poor through education and housing. She was canonized in 2000. Her dedication to the education of children, her example of selflessness and generosity, and the fact that she is a more contemporary saint are reasons for helping young children become acquainted with her. In our consumer society she offers a model of an alternative lifestyle. The children can also be encouraged to become more enthusiastic about learning.

Symbols Mark the Saint

Book: This symbolizes learning, the joy it gives, its importance, and how to share it.

Lessons to Be Learned

- To know that difficult things can be achieved with hard work
- To recognize Saint Katharine Drexel as a recently-canonized saint
- To see how money can be used freely to assist others, without concern for self

Using This Saint

See general instructions common to all the saints (pp.2-5).

As an alternative to *Acting Out the Story*, use the following activity.

Read the story of Saint Katharine. Then have the children each make a book about some things they know. Use eight to ten sheets of white paper (8.5" x 11"). Staple them together to make a book. You can also staple lined paper into the books for writing sentences or stories. Cover the staples with a strip of thick tape, such a duct tape. Have the children label each page with a subject. Choose topics according to age; you may decide on them together with the children. If the children are preschool age, you or your aides can write something across the top of each page; for example, "Jesus," "angel," "love," and so on. If the children are older, you may choose topics such as Jesus, prayer, God, sacraments, saints, and so on. You can also include a "me" page.

Once the pages are labeled, tell the children to write about, draw, or attach things that show what they know on the appropriate pages. For example, for Jesus, have the little ones glue or draw a picture of Jesus; for angel, draw wings or glue cotton balls; for love, glue or draw a picture of someone they love. On the "me" page goes a self-portrait, plus any information they want to share. Encourage the children to make the cover special. Then they can share what they know with someone in the class or at home.

Acting Out the Story

Figures: young Katharine (copy girl from Saint Hildegard; shorten hair, p.56), Katherine as a nun, mother (copy from Maria Goretti, p.101), Native American girl, African American girl

If you choose to use the figures to tell the story, here are some suggestions. Either you or the children can make one or more of each of the figures and attach them to popsicle sticks or dowels. Have the children hold their characters up and put them down at the places indicated in the story. Older children might make the characters act out the "actions"; for example, where the characters in the story are walking, have the figures "walk" (move back and forth); when the characters are talking, have the figures face each other and move up and down slightly; and so on.

Story

Katharine Drexel was the daughter of a very rich family. Her mother and father had so much money, they could buy Katharine anything she wanted. What would you want your mom and dad to buy you if you were rich? (Let the children dream big here!)

Well, do you know what Katharine's parents did with their money? They invited poor people into their home several days a week. They fed them, gave them clothes, and taught them. Can you imagine what it must be like to have a lot of strangers in your house? Do you think Katharine thought it was a waste of money?

No, she did not. She loved helping poor people.

(Hold up young Katharine and Mother) "Mother," said Katharine, "did you see how happy that little girl was just to have a sandwich? I mean, it was just a little ham sandwich and she was crying, Mother! I can have a sandwich any time I want."

"Yes, Katharine, you can," her mother agreed. "Because we have so much money and everything we need, we give what we have to those who have nothing or very little. Do you think your father and I could eat and leave all those starving people out on the street?"

"No, Mother, you couldn't. You and Father are such loving people! I hope I'm as loving as you are when I grow up," said Katharine, hugging her mother.

"You are already, my sweet Katharine," her mother said. "Now, let's finish our work here. There will be more people coming tomorrow." (Put down all figures)

Katharine's mother was right. Katharine already loved those who were in need. When she grew up, she became a nun. (Hold up Katherine as nun) She moved to an area where many poor people lived. She and other women worked especially with Native Americans and African Americans. (Hold up Native American and African American Girls) These were some of the poorest people in America at that time. She opened Catholic schools for African Americans in thirteen states. She started twenty-three rural schools for the poor in farm areas. Fifty Native American missions were also begun by her and the other sisters. She even opened a college called Xavier University. All this cost a lot of money. Where do you think she got all the money to open all these schools and missions? *(Put down all figures)*

You're right. It was her own money. Instead of opening her own home to others, she built homes and schools with her family's money. She spent millions of dollars to help other people. She didn't want any for herself.

When Katharine was a little girl, someone asked her what she wanted most in the world. Do you know what she said?

"I want to help people with all the money my family has given me." That was her big dream, and that is what she did. She helped so many people and made many sacrifices. Katharine especially loved children. She prayed a lot, too. Katharine showed her love for Jesus in many ways. In the year 2000, Katharine Drexel was named a saint.

Prayer

Dear Saint Katharine Drexel, you didn't think of buying things for yourself with all your money. You only thought of helping poor people get things like food and education. Help me be more like you. If someone asks me what I want most, help me learn to think of others, too. Amen.

Words to Know

Wealthy: having lots of money

Missions: places where poor people can go to live and eat and learn

Money: what you use to buy things with

Poor people: people who don't have enough to eat or drink or have a place to live

Education: learning

Katharine as a nun

Jesus
is
love.

Native American girl

Saint Maria Goretti

Why This Saint?

Maria Goretti is the perfect example for today's world of easy choices. She made a difficult decision by focusing on the will of God and not on the world's ways. Her strength, even at such a young age, and the very real threat that she endured are a wonderful example of living a good and pure life.

Lessons to Be Learned

- To introduce the concept of purity
- To teach that even children can choose God first
- To understand what courage means
- To learn about a real girl who made the right choices, despite the consequences

Using This Saint

See general instructions common to all the saints (pp.2-5).

Alternatives to *Acting Out the Story*:

1. Discussing the story with older children can be a powerful reinforcing tool if you are covering the delicate topic of saying no to someone who wants to hurt them. It gives children a language they can practice and use. Discuss also Maria's love for Jesus and Alessandro's conversion.

2. Focus on Maria's love for Jesus and Alessandro's vision and conversion. Use the parable of the Lost Sheep or that of the Prodigal Son to show the children how much joy there is in heaven when one sinner repents. You might make some sheep with cotton and have them put Alessandro's name on one.

Acting Out the Story

Figures: Maria (without the lilies, add them later), Mother, Alessandro

If the "knife" prop is too vivid an image for your age group, don't include it.

Symbols Mark the Saint

The lily: The symbol of purity of which she herself is now an example.

The knife: This represents the ever-present danger to Maria, not only for her physical well-being, but also for her soul.

If you choose to use the figures to tell the story, here are some suggestions. Either you or the children can make one or more of each of the figures and attach them to popsicle sticks or dowels. Have the children hold their characters up and put them down at the places indicated in the story. Older children might make the characters act out the "actions"; for example, where the characters in the story are walking, have the figures "walk" (move back and forth); when the characters are talking, have the figures face each other and move up and down slightly; and so on.

Story

Young Maria Goretti lived in a very small village in Italy. Her family was poor. They loved each other very much. When she was a young girl, her family moved into a different house. It was closer to work for her father, but it was not a very healthy place to live.

Maria's father soon became ill from hard work and the unhealthy living conditions. Soon he died from the illness. *(Hold up Mother and Maria)* Mrs. Goretti had to take in another family to help pay for their house. Maria helped her mother as much as she could. She often walked to church to go to Mass and receive Jesus in Holy Communion. *(Put down Mother and Maria)*

(Hold up Alessandro) The son of the family who lived with the Gorettis, Alessandro, was not a good young man. He liked to do bad things, like stealing. He wasn't good company for Maria. Her mother didn't like to have him in the house with them. But her family was so poor, she didn't have a choice.

(Hold up Maria) Alessandro tried to make Maria do things that she knew were wrong. Maria said, "No!" Maria loved Jesus so much that she wanted to do only what pleased him. She knew that what Alessandro wanted was very wrong. She told him so, but that only made him angry.

"I'll get you, Maria," Alessandro yelled at Maria as she ran into the house. *(Put down Maria and Alessandro)*

One day, Maria was alone at home. The young man tried to force Maria again to do something wrong. This time he said he'd hurt her if she didn't give in. *(Hold up Maria and Alessandro)* Maria was afraid, but she said, "No! It is a sin! God does not want it!" Then the young man stabbed her with a knife and ran away. *(Put down Alessandro)*

(Hold up Mother) Maria was hurt very badly. When her mother came home, she found Maria lying on the floor.

"O, my beautiful Maria! What has happened to you?"

"Mama, it was Alessandro. He wanted me to do something wrong, but I said no. I told him it was a sin. Pray for him, Mama." *(Put down Maria and Mother)*

Friends of the family helped Maria's mother bring her to a hospital. The doctors tried to help Maria, but she was hurt very badly.

(Hold up Maria) The priest brought Maria Holy Communion. "Maria, do you forgive Alessandro?" he asked.

"Yes, Father," Maria said. "I forgive him and pray for him." Then she received Jesus.

(Put down Maria) Maria died soon after. She was only eleven years old. What a brave little girl!

Alessandro was caught by the police and put into prison. For many years he wasn't sorry at all for what he'd done.

(Hold up Alessandro) Alessandro was in prison for years and years. One night, he lay on his little bed. *(Hold up Maria with lilies)* Suddenly, Maria was in his room! He could see her standing right there. And do you know what? She was smiling at him. All around her were lilies, a beautiful flower that is the symbol of purity.

"I am sorry, Maria!" he cried. "I am so sorry!" Alessandro was sad and sorry, but he was thankful, too, for her forgiveness. He felt like a new man. *(Put down all figures)*

When Alessandro was very old and had served his time in prison, he was released. He went to live with monks, holy men, who treated him well. He also went to see Maria's mother. He begged her to forgive him for what he'd done. She said, "My daughter forgave you. Who am I not to forgive you?"

What made Alessandro become a good man? It was love. It was forgiveness. It's not very easy to be kind to someone who hurts you, is it? It's hard to pray for someone who doesn't treat you very well. Maria teaches us that good things come from good.

Maria always tried to do things out of love for God. This is Jesus' way. This is what he asks of us. The Church named Maria a saint in 1950.

Prayer

Dear Saint Maria, help me be courageous like you. Help me say "no" to bad things and "yes" to loving ones. Help me always respond in love, even when something hurts me. Amen.

Words to Know

Symbol: when something stands for something else, like a gold ring for a saint's halo
Purity: keeping yourself sinless in spirit, thinking about and doing good things
Forgiveness: when you don't hold any anger toward someone for hurting you
Prison: a place for people who do bad things that are against the law
Courageous: being brave, even when you're afraid; to choose to do the right thing

Maria

Mother

Alessandro

Saint Francis of Assisi

Why This Saint?

Francis is a dramatic example of how much we can do when we love God. He was a rich and privileged young man. Francis was noted for his carefree lifestyle. Only after experiencing two visions of Jesus did Francis begin to understand that another way of life was intended for him.

Despite his lighthearted approach to life, Francis also had a loving heart. He gave to the poor. He even gave away some of the material goods his father sold. His father wanted Francis to be an important and educated young man. He became angry that Francis only cared about prayer and helping the poor. So he disinherited Francis. Francis was destitute, just the way he wanted it. For him, a life a poverty was the ultimate in simplicity and love of God. Saint Francis is noted for his love for all God's creatures. This is one of his most appealing characteristics for small children, who love little creatures, too.

Symbols Mark the Saint

Package: This represents the fact that Francis had lots of money and could buy anything he wanted.

Deer: The deer symbolizes Francis' care for all God's creatures, and how they responded to him.

Lessons to Be Learned

- To consider poverty of spirit as a blessing
- To practice giving up things as a way of making more room for God in our lives
- To realize that God created all things. We are all connected to God and to each other.

Using This Saint

See general instructions for all the saints (pp.2-5).

Alternatives to *Acting Out the Story*:

1. Read the story, then discuss: How can the children imitate Saint Francis? Both children and adults find it hard to sacrifice things they like. Invite your learners to bring in a toy or book they like, but that they are willing to give away. The donations should be in good condition, and you should have the parents' written approval to do it. When all the toys are collected, take them to an organization that accepts such donations, for example, the Saint

Vincent de Paul Society, or your parish outreach group. If possible, have the children attend the event, so they can see the fruit of their sacrifices.

The Story presents the idea of seeing all creatures as our brothers and sisters. Stressing this idea opens the children's eyes to the reverence we should show toward the gifts God has given us. To illustrate this, have your children select an animal, bird, or fish, or the sun or moon; or even Saint Francis himself. Begin with the following:

"Saint Francis, today we ask you to teach us how to love and care for all God's creatures." Ask the children to say why each one they have chosen is a gift from God.

Acting Out the Story

Figures: young Francis (copy young Anthony, p.10), Mother (copy Anthony's mother, p.12), Father (copy Anthony's father, p.11), Francis as religious brother

If you choose to use the figures to tell the story, here are some suggestions. Either you or the children can make one or more of each of the figures and attach them to popsicle sticks or dowels. Have the children hold their characters up and put them down at the places indicated in the story. Older children might make the characters act out the "actions"; for example, where the characters in the story are walking, have the figures "walk" (move back and forth); when the characters are talking, have the figures face each other and move up and down slightly; and so on.

Story

(Hold up young Francis) Once a very rich young man lived in the city of Assisi, in Italy. If he lived today, he'd be the kid with all the best video games, the latest computers, the most powerful dirt bike, the neatest clothes, the most expensive remote control cars and airplanes, the best stereo, and more. *(Put down Francis)*

Even in Francis' time, some people were envious of him and wanted to be like him because he had everything! But Francis was also generous and enjoyed having fun with his friends.

Yes, Francis had everything a person could want. Do you think all his stuff made Francis happy? Well, sometimes it did, but mostly it didn't.

(Hold up young Francis and Mother) "Francis, why aren't you happy?" asked his mother one day. She loved Francis very much and didn't like to see him unhappy.

"Don't worry about me, Mother," he said with a smile. "Sometimes I just wonder what I really want to do with my life."

"Francis, you know your father would like you to take over his business. Isn't that what you want?"

"I'm not sure, Mother," Francis said. "But I'll know when the time comes." *(Put down Francis and Mother)*

One day, Francis had a vision of Jesus. "Francis!" Jesus said.

"Jesus?" Francis could hardly believe it.

"Yes, Francis. You are meant to do more with your life," Jesus said. "I want you to follow me."

(Hold up Francis as religious brother) So, Francis did just that. He put on clothes made of rough fabric, like the kind poor people wore. He begged for food and a place to stay.

Can you imagine what Francis' mother and father thought? Here was their beautiful and rich son who gave everything he owned to the poor. *(Hold up Father)* His father was hopping mad! First, his father locked him in a room. When he saw Francis wouldn't change his mind, he told Francis never to come home again. Francis was very sad, but in his heart, he knew that his real home was with Jesus. *(Put down Father and Francis)*

Francis began to preach the good message of the gospels. The gospels are the stories in the Bible that tell about the life and teachings of Jesus. In fact, Francis looked to Jesus to be his example. He treated each person as his brother or sister. Francis even called the birds and fish and all animals his brothers and sisters because God had made them, too.

Saint Francis wrote a beautiful poem about creation. He cared for all of God's creatures and the world God created. Do you have any pets at home? Do you take care of them? Are you kind to other animals?

Many young men began to follow Francis. They lived very simple lives, owning nothing of their own. They went from town to town to preach the gospel.

As Francis grew older, he became very sick. The doctors couldn't save him. He died in 1226, in Italy. He was named Saint Francis of Assisi in 1228. He was declared a saint so soon because everyone could see his goodness and love for God.

Prayer

Dear Saint Francis, you gave up all your worldly goods for something better: Love! Help me not to think so much about having more things. Help me see that I am a brother or sister to everyone. I will try to show my love by being as generous as you. Amen.

Words to Know

Expensive: things that cost a lot of money

Satisfy: to have enough to be happy

Preach: to tell people about God and his love for them

Gospel: the good news about Jesus as found in the Bible

Bible: a collection of books that give us God's own word

Poem: a special way of writing that usually rhymes

Francis as a religious brother

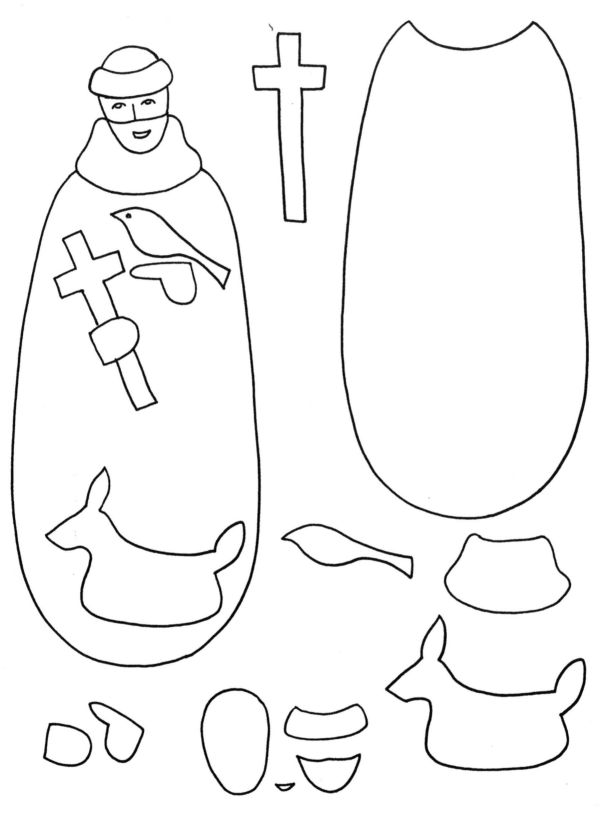

Saint Maximilian Kolbe

Why This Saint?

Countless unnamed saints suffered during the horror known as the Holocaust. Fortunately, we know the stories of a few of them. Maximilian Kolbe's life and death offered in love is one of these.

When Maximilian Kolbe was young, he had a vision of the Blessed Virgin that changed his life. He became a Franciscan priest and started a newspaper that spread devotion to Jesus and Mary. Later, when the German army took over Poland, Maximilian and other priests were sent to the prison camp Auschwitz. While there, Maximilian offered up his life in the place of another man who had a wife and children. Presenting his work as a priest, like your parish priests, can help the children relate to him. Stress also his great love for and imitation of Jesus and Mary.

Symbols Mark the Saint

Miraculous medal: The medal shows the saint's strong love and devotion for the Virgin Mary.

Red crown: This crown represents an acceptance of martyrdom.

White crown: This crown represents an acceptance of a consecrated life.

Lessons to Be Learned

- To be introduced to this saint and his place in history
- To understand better the meaning of martyrdom
- To witness the horrors man can cause when he departs from God's way
- To see love expressed in a selfless way
- To witness faith in action

Using This Saint

See general instructions common to all the saints (pp.2-5).

Acting Out the Story

Figures: young Maximilian (reduce Saint Thérèse's father and copy without beard and cross, p.130), Our Lady (copy from Saint Bernadette, p.28), Maximilian the priest, Maximilian the prisoner, Soldier, Prisoner. Make two crowns: one white, one red.

If you choose to use the figures to tell the story, here are some suggestions. Either you or the children can make one or more of each of the figures and attach them to popsicle sticks or dowels. Have the children hold their characters up and put them down at the places indicated in the story. Older children might make the characters act out the "actions"; for example, where the characters in the story are walking, have the figures "walk" (move back and forth); when the characters are talking, have the figures face each other and move up and down slightly; and so on.

Story

(Hold up young Maximilian) When Maximilian Kolbe was twelve years old, he had a vision. Do you know what a vision is? It's a special gift from God, and a special message just for the person. Isn't that neat?

(Hold up Our Lady) Maximilian saw Mary, our Mother, the Mother of Jesus. He was a little frightened.

"I know who you are, my Lady," said Maximilian. "What do you want of me?" he asked. "What do you want me to do?"

(Hold up two crowns) Mary held out two crowns. One crown was white. The other crown was red. You know what a crown is, don't you? Kings and queens and princes and princesses wear them.

Maximilian knew what the crowns meant. The white crown meant that he should work to be pure, to honor God in all his thoughts and actions. The red crown meant that he would become a martyr. A martyr is someone who is put to death because of his or her belief in Jesus.

What do you think Maximilian did? Maximilian said, "I'll take both." *(Put down all figures)*

(Hold up Maximilian as priest) The young man studied very hard and became a priest. He was such a smart man! He loved Mary so much that he started the Immaculata Movement. This was a special group that helped people love God. They honored Mary, especially by wearing the Miraculous Medal. Maximilian also wrote and printed a special magazine. It helped many people draw closer to Jesus and Mary. *(Put down Maximilian)*

(Hold up Soldier) Then, a terrible war began: World War II. The Nazi soldiers came with guns and tanks. They took over many cities, including the city where Father Maximilian lived and worked. The soldiers did not want people to believe in Jesus or Mary. *(Hold up Maximilian as prisoner)* They took Maximilian to a prison called Auschwitz. The guards treated Maximilian very badly. But this did not stop him from helping people love Mary and Jesus. It didn't matter how hurt Maximilian was. He always helped care for the other people in the prison.

One day, a prisoner escaped. The soldiers were angry! They said, "We're going to kill ten prisoners for the one that escaped." They chose ten men, but one of the men started to cry.

(Hold up Prisoner) "No, no, don't kill me, please," he begged. "I have a wife and children! Please, don't kill me. Who will take care of them?"

Then Father Maximilian spoke. "Please let me take his place," he said.

The commander of the soldiers told Maximilian to step forward. Maximilian prayed he would let the other man go. The commander stared into Maximilian's eyes.

"You want to die in his place?" he asked, pointing to the other man.

"Yes, I do," Maximilian said.

"Very well, it's your choice," said the soldier.

"Get up," he said to the man. "The priest has offered to take your place."

The man was grateful but also ashamed. He knew that Father Maximilian was a loving man. He didn't want Maximilian to die, either. *(Put down all figures)*

Maximilian smiled and nodded. This meant that everything was going to be all right. Maximilian and the other nine men were put into a prison cell and left to die. They were not given any water or food. Through it all, Maximilian prayed and sang hymns with them. He helped them keep strong in their faith. Finally, Maximilian was the last man left alive. The soldiers could not believe it.

(Hold up Maximilian and Soldier) "How can he still be alive? It's been three weeks! No one can stay alive that long," they said. *(Hold up two crowns)* Maximilian just prayed to Mary and Jesus. In his mind, he saw the white crown on his head. Above the white crown was the red crown.

"Give him the shot of poison now!" shouted the leader. They gave Maximilian a shot of poison in his arm, and he died. Before he died, he saw the red crown float down onto his head. He was a martyr for God. *(Put down all figures)*

Maximilian was named a saint in 1982. The man for whom he gave his life was at the ceremony.

Prayer

Dear Saint Maximilian Kolbe, sometimes I am afraid. I want to have courage like you. Help me to be loving and generous as you were. Show me how to be good and pure. Amen.

Words to Know

Martyr: someone who is put to death because of his or her belief in Jesus

Miraculous Medal: a special medal worn to honor Mary and her Son, Jesus

Prison: a place where people are kept for punishment

Poison: a liquid or powder that hurts the body, sometimes killing the body

Maximilian the priest

Maximillian the prisoner

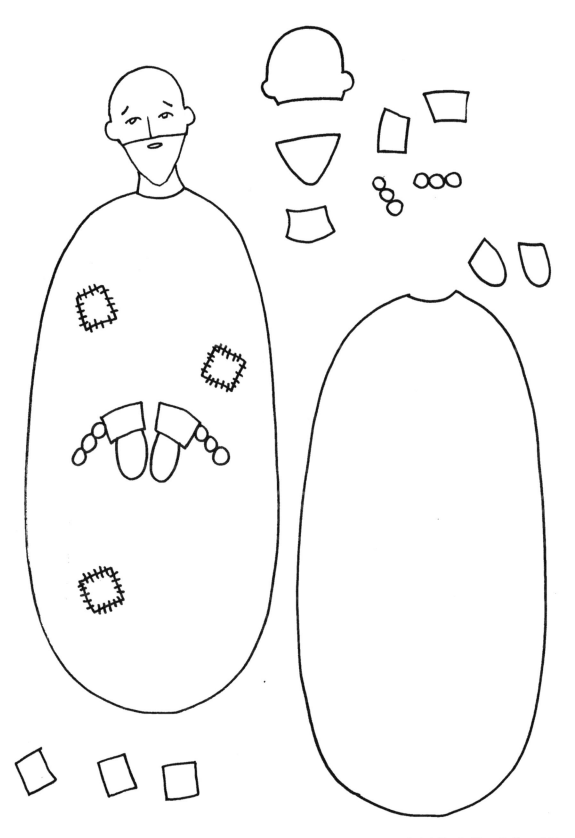

Prisoner

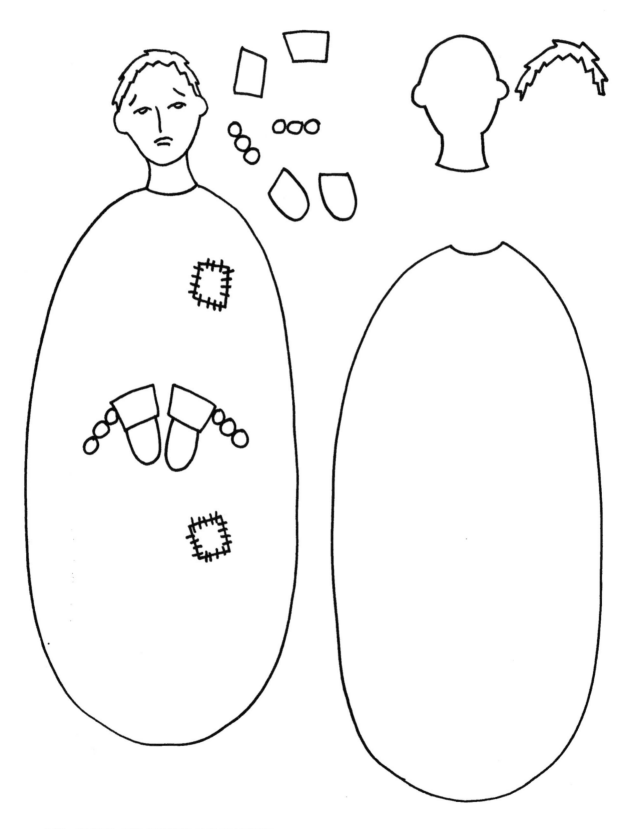

Soldier

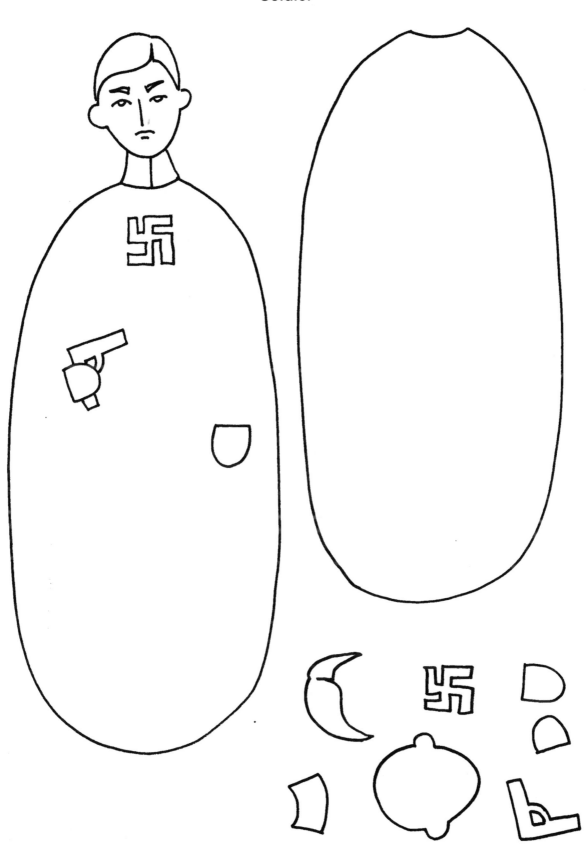

Saint Peter

Symbols Mark the Saint

Fishing Pole: Saint Simon Peter was the great fisher of men.

Boat: The boat represents being cast adrift, left alone.

Fish: When Jesus spoke of being "fishers of men," the fish symbolized man; for early Christians it was also a symbol for Jesus.

Simon Peter: When Jesus called a person to follow him, he often changed their name. Names can represent what we do or become.

Why This Saint?

So often people think of saints as meek and mild, without any passions. Like anyone else, saints can endure sufferings that might lead them away from their love of God. Simon Peter knew Jesus, and that is a remarkable thing to contemplate! He was Jesus' friend, but sometimes he wasn't a very good friend. Simon Peter is a fantastic example to show children that we must persevere. God often chooses the weak to fulfill his greatest missions. Saint Peter was our first pope.

Lessons to Be Learned

- To study Saint Peter's own behavior: how he professes unconditional faith one minute and sinks into the water the next; how he swears he'll die with Jesus, then denies he knows him

- To be made aware of the great mystery of God's love, of Jesus' love, despite the way we act

- To understand that God's plan and love are mysteries to us

Using This Saint

See general instructions common for all the saints (pp.2-5).

An alternative to *Acting Out the Story*: Read the story of Saint Peter. Talk about the changes in his behavior; e.g., he has faith and walks on the water; then suddenly he becomes afraid and starts to sink. Encourage the children to think of changes in their own behavior. For example, one little girl may have pledged her friendship to another girl, until a third came along. A boy may be chosen for a particular sports team, then is told someone else is wanted instead. Discuss how these are hurtful. What can they do about it?

Acting Out the Story

Figures: Peter the fisherman (without keys, but with rod and fish), Jesus, Peter with keys, boat Use a square or round dowel or even a pencil to make the fishing pole, along with a length of thread. Magnets glued to the end of the fishing line and the back of the fish can make "fishing" fun for your children. If you want a three-dimensional boat, you can use a plastic milk jug cut to the right shape. A tissue box covered with brown construction paper also serves the purpose.

If you choose to use the figures to tell the story, here are some suggestions. Either you or the children can make one or more of each of the figures and attach them to popsicle sticks or dowels. Have the children hold their characters up and put them down at the places indicated in the story. Older children might make the characters act out the "actions"; for example, where the characters in the story are walking, have the figures "walk" (move back and forth); when the characters are talking, have the figures face each other and move up and down slightly; and so on.

Story

(Hold up Peter the fisherman) A long time ago lived a man named Simon, who was a fisherman by trade. Simon was a happy man. One day, while Simon and his brother Andrew were casting their net into the lake, a man came up to them. The man said to him, "You are fishermen, but come with me and I will make you fishers of men."

(Hold up Jesus) The man was Jesus. Simon and Andrew dropped their fishing net onto the beach and walked right after Jesus. Just like that.

Simon became Jesus' friend. For three years he walked with him, learned from him, and was challenged by him to become what God planned. But Simon didn't always do the right thing. Sometimes he became very angry. Sometimes he wanted to do things his own way and not Jesus' way. But one thing was certain. Simon loved Jesus with all his heart. *(Put Peter and Jesus down)*

So, what did Jesus mean when he said he'd make Simon a fisher of men? Think about what Jesus did while he was on earth. Through stories called parables Jesus taught them what God is like, what God's kingdom is like, what path we are to follow. This story about Saint Simon shows you just what he was like.

(Hold up Peter "in" boat) One day, Simon and the rest of the apostles—they were other close followers of Jesus—were in a large boat fishing. A huge storm came up and it was dark outside. Lightning was flashing and striking the sea. The boat bounced up and down and up and down on the waves. The thunder was so loud that the apostles couldn't hear each other scream. The rain pelted them with little stings like bees. Do you know what happened then? The apostles saw something moving toward them on the water.

"What is that, Simon?" shouted Andrew. They were all so scared.

(Hold up Jesus) "It's Jesus!" shouted Simon to the rest of the apostles.

"It can't be Jesus," said Thomas. "Whatever is walking on top of the water is coming right toward us." All the apostles were screaming! Then they heard a familiar voice say, "Stop worrying. It is I, Jesus." But the apostles weren't sure. After all, how could Jesus walk on the water? So they kept screaming, "It's a ghost! It's a ghost!"

Simon was watching Jesus walking on the water. He shouted out to him, "Jesus, if it's really you, tell me to walk out to you on the water!"

Jesus said, "Simon, come out to me." *(Peter gets out of boat and moves toward Jesus)* So Simon stepped out of the rocking boat and do you know what? He stood on top of the water just as if he were on the land. He just kept staring at Jesus and walking toward him. But then something happened! Simon stopped looking at Jesus and started looking around him at the storm, the lightning, and the rain. Simon said to himself, "I can't be walking on the water." And guess what? Of course! *(Peter starts to sink)* In the deep sea, in the dark, during a huge storm, Simon was sinking into the water. He didn't know how to swim. He yelled out, "Jesus, save me!" Immediately Jesus reached out his hand and grabbed Simon. Then Jesus and Simon climbed into the boat. The storm died down very quickly. The apostles couldn't believe what they had just seen.

"Simon," asked Jesus, "why did you stop believing?" Simon didn't know what to say or think except, "Jesus, you are the Son of God!" *(Put down all figures)*

One day, Jesus said to Simon, *(Hold up Jesus and Peter with keys)* "Your name is now going to be Peter which means rock. If you want to build a good, strong building that doesn't fall into the ground or get washed away by the sea, you build it on solid rock. So, you are Peter, and on this Rock I am going to build my Church," said Jesus. *(Put down Jesus and Peter)*

How can Peter be a Rock? How can Jesus build a Church on Peter? Well, because Jesus' Church is not a building. Jesus' Church is in our hearts. Jesus knew it would take a very strong person to lead his Church. So he chose Peter to be the first pope, the leader of Jesus' Church, our Church. Do you know who the pope is now?

Prayer

Dear Saint Peter, Jesus knew that you made mistakes sometimes. But you still did great things for Jesus. Help me think of Jesus often. May everything I do be a great thing for Jesus. Help me be a fisher of men by being a good boy or girl. Help me be strong, so I can do the right thing. Amen.

Words to Know

Fisherman: someone who fishes for a living

Challenge: when something pushes you to do better

Plan: when you decide how to get something done

Parable: a story that has hidden meaning

Apostles: the first followers of Jesus, the men Jesus chose to follow him

Pope: the leader of the Catholic Church

Peter the fisherman/with keys

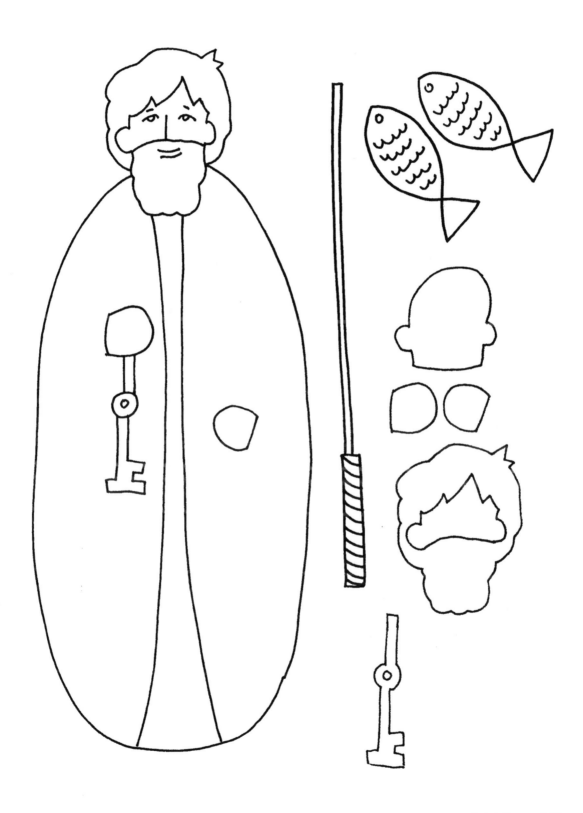

Peter's robe

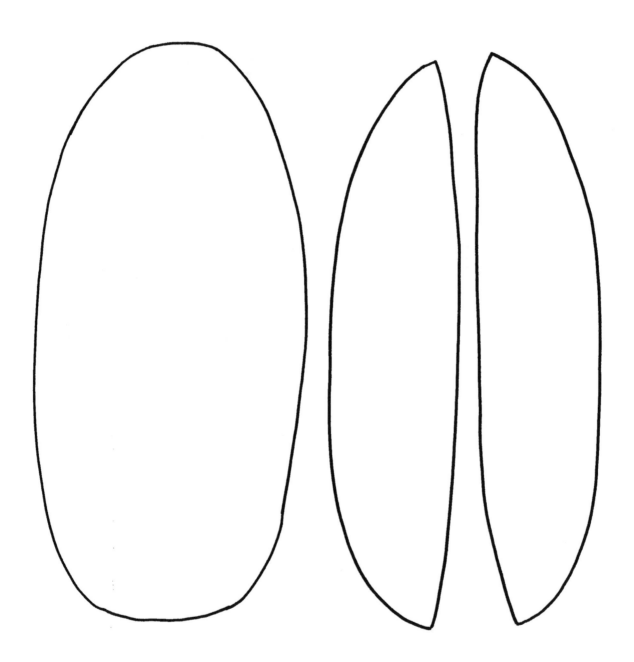

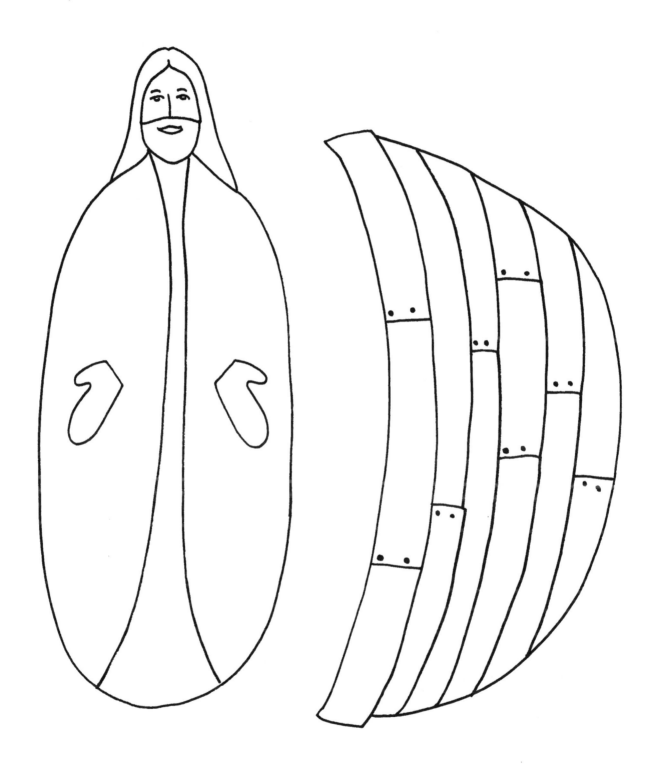

Jesus

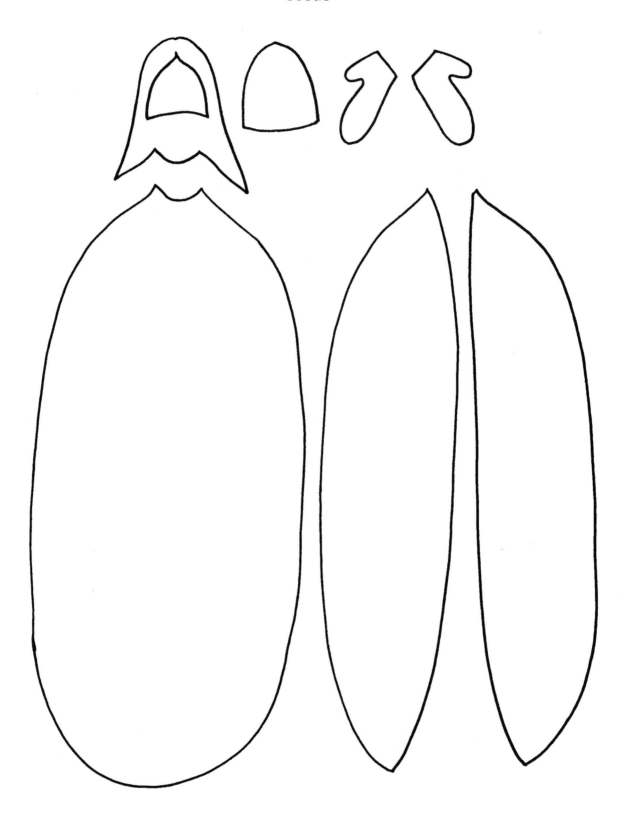

Blessed Mother Teresa of Calcutta

Why This Saint?

Mother Teresa is perhaps one of the most recognized persons in the world. However, very young children may not know her. Even while she lived, people knew she was a holy person. Her selfless love shown through her care for the poor in India is well documented. For your children, the importance of this saint lies especially in her prayer life and her selfless care for others through her work with the poorest of people.

Lessons to Be Learned

- To discover that there are people in the world today who do not have enough to eat or a bed to sleep in or even water to wash with

- To learn that prayer can strengthen and help us through the day

- To persevere in obedience as well as in listening to God's voice

- To learn that real giving means going beyond what is extra, giving up what you want

Symbols Mark the Saint

White sari: The sari represents the common dress of Indian women; Mother Teresa did not wish to separate herself from people but to show she was one of them.

Blue stripes: The color blue is in honor of Mary, our Mother.

Bowl of rice: This shows that we can give even when we don't have much.

Using This Saint

See general instructions common for all the saints (pp.2-5).

As an alternative to *Acting Out the Story*, the children might enjoy reenacting the rice story. Instead of rice, start out with a big bowl of popcorn. Read the story. Then ask the children to pretend the popcorn is their meal for the day. Show them how much there is. They will feel pretty certain they have more than enough. Divide it in half, then in half again, then again. Continue until there is very little left per person. Remind them about the part of the story about the Indian woman who gave half of her rice to her starving friend, even though her children were very hungry, too. You can compare this to the gospel example where Jesus praises the poor widow who puts two coins into the offering box (Luke 21:1–4).

Acting Out the Story

Figures: Sister Teresa (copy Saint Thérèse without roses and cross, p.131), Bishop (copy from Juan Diego, p.83), Mother Teresa, Buhkti

If you choose to use the figures to tell the story, here are some suggestions. Either you or the children can make one or more of each of the figures and attach them to popsicle sticks or dowels. Have the children hold their characters up and put them down at the places indicated in the story. Older children might make the characters act out the "actions"; for example, where the characters in the story are walking, have the figures "walk" (move back and forth); when the characters are talking, have the figures face each other and move up and down slightly; and so on.

Story

Mother Teresa was never a mother, that is, she never had any children of her own. But people all over the world call her mother. Do you know why? Because mothers take care of their children. People all over the world felt that Mother Teresa was taking care of them.

(Hold up Sister Teresa) Teresa became a nun when she was eighteen years old. Agnes was her baptismal name. For a long time, she was a teacher. Later she believed God was calling her to live with and care for some of the very poorest people in the world, in India. So Teresa went to the bishop to ask his permission.

(Hold up Bishop) "Bishop," asked Teresa, "I wish to move into the poor hovels in the slums of India."

"Why? Why would you leave your nice bed and good food to live where it smells. There are many diseases," said the bishop.

"Because that is where I'm needed the most, Bishop. I can help the people there. I can teach them to care for themselves. I can teach them to read. Most of all, I can tell them about Jesus' love for them," Sister Teresa replied.

The bishop didn't want to lose Sister Teresa, but he believed what she was saying was true. "All right, Sister Teresa, you may leave your convent and live as you request. God bless you in your work," he said. *(Put down Teresa and Bishop)*

Teresa did not want to wear her habit in the slums. She decided to wear the kind of dress that Indian women wear, called a sari. Teresa added some blue stripes to the sari to remind her of our Blessed Mother Mary.

For many years, Teresa helped the poor. She taught them hygiene. She taught them how to read and write by using the dirt on the ground for a chalkboard. And she taught them to love Mary and Jesus.

Other young woman came to work with Teresa. She was then called Mother Teresa.

(Hold up Mother Teresa and Buhkti) One day, Mother Teresa made a bowl of rice for a woman named Buhkti, whose husband had just died. The poor woman had eight children and no food. So, Mother Teresa walked with this big bowl of rice to the hovel that the woman and her eight children lived in.

"I am so sorry to hear about the death of your husband," said Mother Teresa as she put down the bowl of rice on a stool near the floor. "He is with God now," she said.

"Yes, Mother Teresa, I know he is with God. I miss him very much, but I know that Jesus continues to take care of me and our children. Look how he cares for me! He lets you come into my home with food!" Buhkti gave Mother Teresa a big hug.

(Have both figures "walk" to another place) Then the woman did something very curious. She picked up the bowl of rice and went outside. Mother Teresa followed her. Buhkti went to the door of the next hovel and pushed it gently with the toe of her sandal. When the door opened, Mother Teresa could see another woman inside that hovel. Around her were several young children.

"Hello, Marat," said Buhkti. "See, I have come with food for you and your children!" She walked over to a low table and scooped half of the rice into a large empty platter that was there. Then she smiled at Marat and left the hovel. Mother Teresa followed.

(Have figures "walk" back) When they were back at Buhkti's hovel, Mother Teresa said, "I see that you follow what Jesus taught very well, Buhkti. You give not only from your heart but from what you need. There was no extra rice in that bowl. You and your children could have eaten that food for two days instead of one. But you thought of your neighbor as yourself."

Then Mother Teresa hugged Buhkti again and smiled as she walked out the door. *(Put down Mother Teresa and Buhkti)*

Mother Teresa was beatified in 2003.

Prayer

Dear Mother Teresa, teach me to give as Buhkti did, as you did all your life. When I have a chance to give something to a needy person, help me do it generously and with all my heart. Amen.

Words to Know

Bishop: a priest who has been called and ordained to lead and serve other priests and people of a diocese

Disease: sickness

Convent: a place where nuns live

Nun: a woman who gives her life and life's work to Jesus

Habit: a uniform that nuns wear

Slums: where many poor people live

Hovel: a hut or poor home

Mother Teresa

Buhkti

Saint Thérèse of Lisieux

Symbols Mark the Saint

Fancy dress: This shows that Thérèse Martin grew up with many comforts.

Habit: The habit symbolizes Thérèse's vocation in the Carmelite order.

Rose: Saint Thérèse said she would send roses once she was in heaven. Many prayers have been answered through her intercession. She has often responded by sending roses, too.

Why This Saint?

Considered the greatest saint of modern times, Saint Thérèse is well known as the Little Flower. Her "Little Way" has drawn thousands of souls to God, as she knew it would. By doing every small thing out of love for God, you, too, may become a saint. Thérèse is an inspiration for children because her childlike confidence in God's love transformed her into an example of doing the ordinary with an extraordinary love.

Lessons to Be Learned

• To understand that God is love and desires love from each of us

• To see that the least important persons and the smallest actions, when filled with love, are as great in God's eyes as the most famous martyrs or theologians

• To look to God for our needs and thank him for everything

Using This Saint

See general instructions common for all the saints (pp.2-5).

As an alternative to *Acting Out the Story*, you might find that role playing scenes from Thérèse's life is enlightening for older children. First read the story. Then, encourage the children to act out scenes from the story that teach them how to respond with a smile or not to defend yourself. This activity helps the children apply the example of the saint to their own lives.

Acting Out the Story

Figures: young Thérèse, Father, Thérèse as nun, flowers in baskets. Optional: old nun (copy Thérèse but put frown on and take away cross and roses)

If you choose to use the figures to tell the story, here are some suggestions. Either you or the children can make one or more of each of the figures and attach them to popsicle sticks or dowels. Have the children hold their characters up and put them down at the places indicated in the story. Older children might make the characters act out the "actions"; for example, where the characters in the story are walking, have the figures "walk" (move back and forth); when the characters are talking, have the figures face each other and move up and down slightly; and so on.

Story

(*Hold up young Thérèse*) Once there was a little girl named Thérèse Martin. When Thérèse was four years old, her mother died. Thérèse missed her very much.

(*Hold up Father*) "Daddy," said Thérèse, crying in her father's arms, "I miss mommy so much! My heart hurts!"

"My little Queen, I miss your mother, too. But she is with God and the angels now. She loves you! Can't you feel her love?"

"Yes, but I want her to hug me like she always did!" Thérèse cried.

"Oh, Thérèse, I will hug you, and your sisters will hug you, until your mother can hug you in heaven." (*Put down Thérèse and Father*)

Thérèse loved Jesus very much. When she was three years old, she used to sit quietly and just think of God. It made her so happy.

But, Thérèse was not always a good girl. As the baby of the family she was a little spoiled. Do you know what spoiled means? Is it fun to be around someone who's spoiled?

"I need someone to dress me," she would say. But when she was a little older, Thérèse realized how she was acting and decided that it didn't make Jesus happy. So she changed! She became a good and loving girl out of love for Jesus.

Thérèse wanted to be a Carmelite nun. She was only fifteen years old when she asked to become a nun. She was too young. She wanted to follow Jesus so much that she even begged the pope to let her join. After a while Jesus granted her desire. On Monday, April 9, 1888, Thérèse Martin became Sister Thérèse. She was so happy!

(*Hold up Thérèse as nun*) How could Sister Thérèse show God how much she loved him? She didn't do things very well. Her sewing was mediocre. (*Hold up flowers in baskets*) She didn't know anything about gardening. One day, Sister Thérèse pulled out all the flowers instead of the weeds. Even during prayers she would fall asleep. However, she always worked very hard to do her best in everything she did. (*Put down Thérèse and baskets*)

Sister Thérèse wondered if God would be happy with her not being the best in anything. Would God be happy with her little chores? Would God be happy with her sewing? Her gardening? Her cleaning? Her praying?

Sister Thérèse thought about this for a long time. If she couldn't do big things, God must be pleased with the little things she did, as long as she did them with great love. Sister Thérèse called this the Little Way. Sister Thérèse did every stitch of sewing with love. She pulled every weed with love. Sister Thérèse thought of Jesus with every prayer she said, every dish she washed, every floor she swept. She did each chore with love for him. In doing this, she grew to love all people, too!

(Hold up old Nun) There was a sister who lived in the same house as Sister Thérèse and who was always complaining. Do you know anyone who is always crabby?

This nun complained about everything. "The water is too cold! There is a draft! You aren't feeding me fast enough! You're feeding me too slowly!" The other nuns, including Sister Thérèse, just didn't want to be around this sister very much. *(Hold up Thérèse as nun)* Then, Sister Thérèse remembered the Little Way. She could show great love in doing small things for this nun. *(Move Thérèse close to old nun)* So she would help her walk to the bathroom and to her room. She helped her eat her dinner and even sat with her while they sewed. In this way, Sister Thérèse was showing love for someone who wasn't easy to love. *(Put down Thérèse and old nun)*

One day, Sister Thérèse caught a very serious disease called tuberculosis. In those days, people did not usually recover from this sickness. There wasn't any cure. For months Sister Thérèse suffered. She died when she was just twenty-four years old.

Everyone who knew Sister Thérèse was very sad. But they didn't know how much she loved God. Very few people had any idea how she had been growing in love every day. No one knew how much her Little Way pleased Jesus. After Thérèse died, they read about her life in a book she had written. Then everyone knew that Sister Thérèse was a very holy woman.

In 1923, the Church named Sister Thérèse a saint. Her book, *The Story of A Soul*, is still being read today. It inspires people all over the world to lead holy lives through little acts done with great love.

Prayer

Dear Saint Thérèse, please help me remember that each thing I do, if I do it with lots of love, makes Jesus very happy. When I clean up my toys, let me think of Jesus smiling. When I brush my teeth, help me think of Jesus' love. When I obey, help me see Jesus saying, "Yes!" Please send me a rose of love. Amen.

Words to Know

Spoiled: when you always want your way and do not think of any one else

Nun: a woman who gives her life and life's work to God

Emergency: when something very serious happens

Gardening: planting flowers and vegetables and taking care of the grass

Draft: cold air that blows in from outside

Tuberculosis: a disease that makes it hard to breathe

Holy: a person is holy when they think and do everything for God

Chores: little jobs, like making your bed, putting your toys away, and washing dishes

Young Thérèse

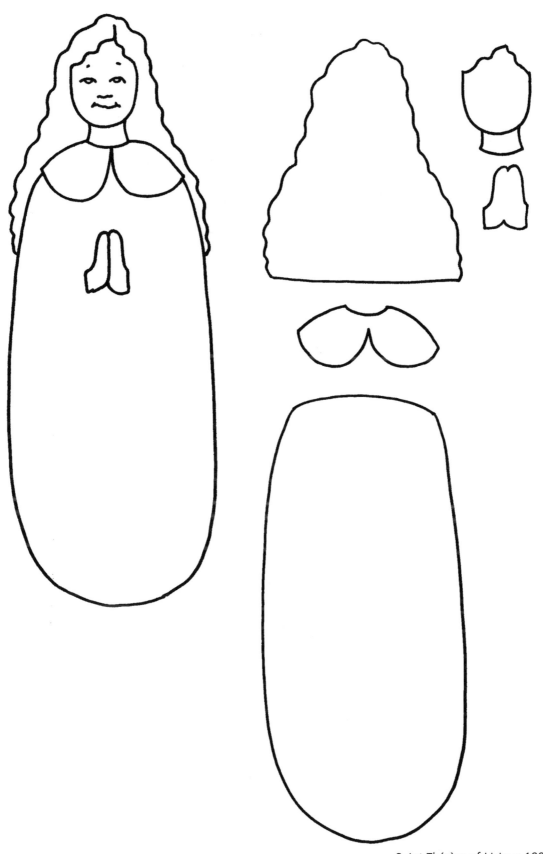

Thérèse's Father

Thérèse as a nun

Holy Abraham and Sarah

Why These Saints?

Often, we think of saints as persons who lived after Jesus. However, holy people were prevalent in the Old Testament as well. What better story could there be for young children than that of elderly parents who longed for a child. The life of holy Abraham and Sarah are about faith, about belief in God's messengers, and about a love that goes beyond selfish needs.

Lessons to Be Learned

- To relate more to persons in the Old Testament

- To understand that God is an active part of our lives, as our creator and our teacher

- To grow in our trust in God, no matter what happens in our lives

Using These Saints

See general instructions common for all the saints (pp.2-5).

As an alternative to *Acting Out the Story*, read the story to the children. Make the figures together. Then have the children act out their own version of the story. You will see which parts or lessons of the story impressed them.

Acting Out the Story

Figures: Abraham, Sarah, Isaac, Angel

If you choose to use the figures to tell the story, here are some suggestions. Either you or the children can make one or more of each of the figures and attach them to popsicle sticks or dowels. Have the children hold their characters up and put them down at the places indicated in the story. Older children might make the characters act out the "actions"; for example, where the characters in the story are walking, have the figures "walk" (move back and forth); when the characters are talking, have the figures face each other and move up and down slightly; and so on.

Story

(Hold up Abraham and Sarah) Sarah was the wife of Abraham. They lived a very long time ago. Sarah and Abraham were elderly people. They never had any children, and that made them sad.

"Abraham, how I wish I had a little baby I could love. I have loved you so well, but a baby is the one thing in my life I have missed," said Sarah to Abraham one day.

"My beautiful Sarah, a child would have made both of us so happy! But it was not meant to be. Let us be happy in our love for each other," replied Abraham. He wanted to make Sarah feel better.

(Put down Sarah) One day, God spoke to Abraham.

"Abraham!" The ground shook. Abraham was afraid, but he answered the voice.

"Yes, I am Abraham."

"I am God, the one, true God. There is no other God before me."

Abraham did not understand. People of that time believed that there were gods for everything: for wind and rain, for growing crops and having children. But on this day, God told Abraham that there was only one God, and that he was God.

"I don't understand, God, but I believe you. I will tell my wife, Sarah." So he went back to their tent and told Sarah what had happened.

(Hold up Sarah) "This voice told me with such authority that he was God, the one, true God, Sarah," Abraham said. "I believe him."

"Abraham, you have never lied to me. I believe you. I believe that there is one God." Then, they both trusted God with all their hearts. They were the first to know and love God just the way we do today. *(Put down both figures)*

Abraham and Sarah were nomads. They had flocks of animals and had to keep finding food and water for them. Abraham and Sarah lived in tents that they could just roll up and move anytime they wanted. They slept on mats on the ground and drank from wells or streams. They traveled all over the desert.

(Hold up Angel) One special day three angels were traveling near Abraham's tent. *(Hold up Abraham)* Abraham greeted them with honor and invited them to have a meal. While they ate, they said to Abraham, "Where is your wife Sarah?"

Abraham answered, "She is in the tent."

One of the angels said, "Your wife Sarah will soon have a son."

(Hold up Sarah) Sarah was listening from inside the tent. When she heard what the angel said, she laughed to herself. She thought God was playing a joke on her.

The angel said, "Is anything too wonderful for God to do? I promise that Sarah will have a son." *(Put down all figures)*

Nine months later, Sarah had a baby boy just as the angel said she would! She trusted God, and God did what God promised. Do you know what Sarah named her son? She named him Isaac. Do you know what Isaac means? Laughter!

How Abraham and Sarah loved their little son Isaac! He was a good boy. He loved his mother and father, too. When Isaac was about nine or ten, the angel came back and spoke to Abraham.

(Hold up Angel and Abraham) "Abraham, God wants you to prove you love him more than you love anyone else. You are to take Isaac to the mountains. There you will build an altar and sacrifice your son to show how much you love God." *(Put down Angel)*

Abraham couldn't breathe. What a hard thing God was asking him to do! But Abraham knew he loved God even more than his own beautiful son. *(Hold up Isaac)* So he said to Isaac, "Isaac, get your robe. We're going up to the mountain, just the two of us." Boy, was Isaac excited about going on a trip with his father!

(Abraham and Isaac "walk" up mountain, then move around as though building altar) They walked and walked up the hill until Abraham found a place that was just perfect for the sacrifice. He asked Isaac to gather some rocks. Together, they built the altar. Isaac had no idea what God had told Abraham to do. *(Put down Abraham and Isaac)*

Abraham hugged Isaac and told him to lie down on the altar. Isaac knew then that his father was going to sacrifice him. He loved his father so much that he didn't say anything. He could see in his father's tears that he didn't want to kill him. Isaac believed his father must have a good reason. So he prayed that God would help him be brave.

(Hold up Abraham; Isaac is lying on top of a box or desk) Abraham raised his arm high in the air with the knife. Before he could bring it down on Isaac, *(Hold up Angel)* the angel appeared and stopped him.

"Abraham, God does not require this sacrifice. He only wanted to test you, to see if you were willing to sacrifice your beloved son for love of God," explained the angel. Then he disappeared. *(Put down Angel)* Abraham gathered Isaac into his arms and cried. He thanked God for letting him keep Isaac. Together Isaac and Abraham walked back down the mountain into the loving arms of Sarah. *(Put down Abraham and Isaac)*

Prayer

Dear Abraham and Sarah, teach me to believe in God the way you did. You became the father and mother of all who believe that God is the one, true God. Teach me to live as you lived. May I be full of laughter and trust and love for God. Amen.

Words to Know

Nomads: people who move from place to place and live in the desert in tents

Believe: to trust that something is so

Impossible: something that, by human standards, can never happen

Trust: to believe, to have confidence in

Universe: a space bigger than the earth, bigger than the solar system, bigger than we can imagine! All the stars, all the planets, all the black holes—everything. Except God!

Abraham

Sarah (with baby Isaac)

Angel

Issac

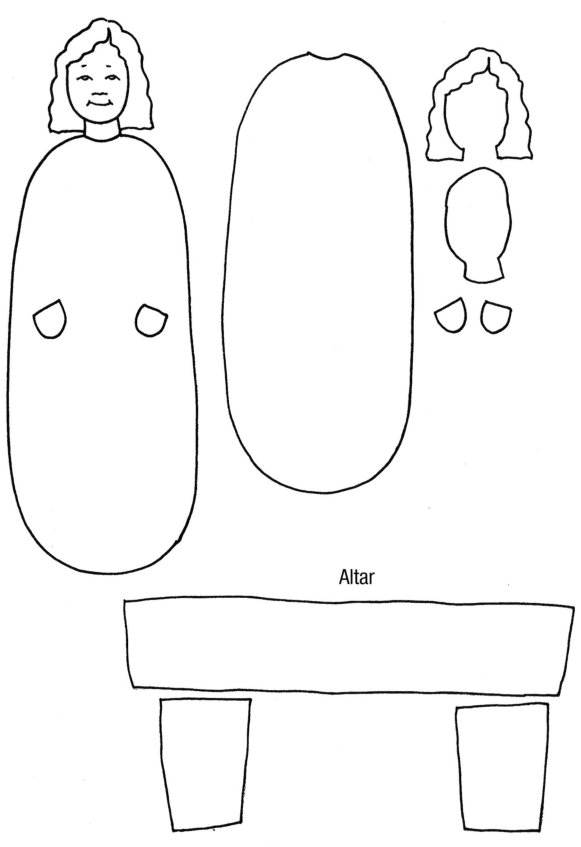

Altar